Travellers' **Russian**

David Ellis is Director of the Somerset Language Centre and co-author of a number of language books.

Anna Pilkington was born in Russia but came to Britain six years ago. She now teaches Russian at Queen Mary's College, London University.

GW00690060

Other phrase books in the series

Travellers' **Dutch**
Travellers' **French**
Travellers' **German**
Travellers' **Greek**
Travellers' **Italian**
Travellers' **Japanese**
Travellers' **Portugese**
Travellers' **Scandinavian**
Travellers' **Serbo-Croat**
Travellers' **Spanish**
Travellers' **Turkish**
Travellers' **Multilingual Phrase Book**

Travellers' **Russian**

David Ellis

Anna Pilkington

Pan Books London, Sydney and Auckland

First published 1990 by Pan Books Ltd
Cavaye Place, London SW10 9PG

9 8 7 6 5 4 3 2 1

ISBN 0 330 31255 3

Phototypeset by Transcommunications Ltd,
Melton Mowbray, Leicester

Printed and bound in Great Britain by
Richard Clay Ltd, Bungay, Suffolk

Contents

Using the phrase book

- This phrase book is designed to help you get by in Russia, to get what you want or need. It concentrates on the simplest but most effective way you can express these needs in an unfamiliar language.
- The **Contents** on p. 5 give you a good idea of which section to consult for the phrase you need.
- The **Index** on p. 125 gives you more detailed information about where to look for your phrase.
- When you have found the right page you will be given:
  either – the exact phrase
  or – help in making up a suitable sentence
  and – help in getting the pronunciation right.
- The English sentences in **bold type** will be useful for you in a variety of different situations, so they are worth learning by heart.
- Wherever possible you will find help in understanding what Russian people say to you in reply to your questions.
- Note especially these three sections:
  Everyday expressions, p. 13
  Shop talk, p. 48
  Public notices, p. 107.
  You are sure to want to refer to them most frequently.
- Once abroad, remember to make good use of the local tourist offices (see p. 26).

UK address:
Soviet Tourist and Information Office,
Intourist House,
219 Marsh Wall,
Isle of Dogs,
London E14 9SJ
Tel: 01-538 8600

A note on the pronunciation system

Russian is not very difficult to pronounce. Only a few sounds do not have a corresponding one in English.

Stress is very important as the meaning of the word can change depending on where stress falls. As an aid the syllables to be stressed are in italics.

For the sake of convenience we have used the following symbols for transcription of the sounds that do not exist in English:

Ж	ж	is transcribed as **zh**
Х	х	is transcribed as **kh**
Ч	ч	is transcribed as **ch**
Ь	ь	usually softens the consonant it follows and is therefore shown as an apostrophe (') after that consonant.
Ы	ы	is transcribed as **y**

Unstressed **o** is normally pronounced as **a**
and unstressed **e** as **i** in pit.

The alphabet

Printed		Handwritten		Pronunciation
А	а	*Ѧ*	*а*	a as in father
Б	б	*Б*	*б*	b as in but
В	в	*В*	*в*	v as in van
Г	г	*Г*	*г*	g as in guess
Д	д	*Д*	*д*	d as in dress
Е	е	*Е*	*е*	ye as in yellow
Ё	ё	*Ё*	*ё*	ya as in yacht
Ж	ж	*Ж*	*ж*	s as in pleasure
З	з	*З*	*з*	z as in zoo
И	и	*И*	*и*	i as in indigo
Й	й	*Й*	*й*	y as in may
К	к	*К*	*к*	c as in class
Л	л	*Л*	*л*	l as in love
М	м	*М*	*м*	m as in mother
Н	н	*Н*	*н*	n as in no
О	о	*О*	*о*	a as in all
П	п	*П*	*п*	p as in plot
Р	р	*Р*	*р*	like Scottish r
С	с	*С*	*с*	s as in smile
Т	т	*Т*	*т*	t as in tent
У	у	*У*	*у*	like u in bull
Ф	ф	*Ф*	*ф*	f as in fun
Х	х	*Х*	*х*	ch as in Scottish loch
Ц	ц	*Ц*	*ц*	ts as in its
Ч	ч	*Ч*	*ч*	ch as in chicken
Ш	ш	*Ш*	*ш*	sh as in fish
Щ	щ	*Щ*	*щ*	s as in sure
Ъ	ъ	*ъ*	*ъ*	hard sign – has no sound of its own but affects other sounds
Ы	ы	*ы*	*ы*	like i in will
Ь	ь	*ь*	*ь*	soft sign – has no sound of its own but affects other sounds
Э	э	*Э*	*э*	like e in bet
Ю	ю	*Ю*	*ю*	yu as in Yugoslavia
Я	я	*Я*	*я*	ya as in yard

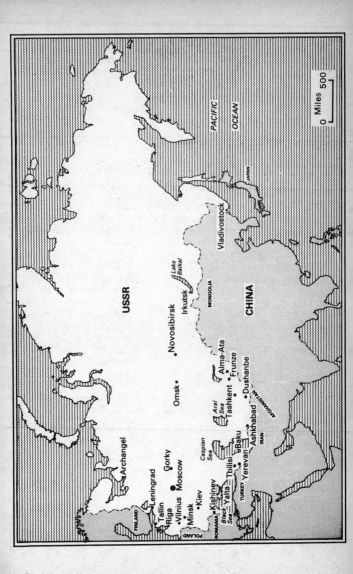

Everyday expressions

[*See also 'Shop talk', p. 48*]

Hello	**Здравствуйте**
	zdrastvuite
Good morning	**Доброе утро**
	dobraye utra
Good day	**Добрый день**
Good afternoon	dobryi dyen
Good evening	**Добрый вечер**
	dobryi vyechir
Good night	**Спокойной ночи**
	spakoinai nochi
Goodbye	**До свидания**
	da-svidan'ya
See you later	**До скорого**
	da-skorava
Yes	**Да**
	da
Please	**Пожалуйста**
	pazhalusta
Yes, please	**Да, пожалуйста**
	da, pazhalusta
Great	**Отлично**
	atlichna
Thank you	**Спасибо**
	spasiba
Thank you very much	**Большое спасибо**
	bal'shoye spasiba
That's right	**Правильно**
	pravil'na
No	**Нет**
	nyet
No, thank you	**Нет, спасибо**
	nyet spasiba
I disagree	**Я не согласен (согласна)**
	Ya ni saglasin (saglasna)
Excuse me	**Извините**
	izvinitye

Sorry	**Простите**
	prast*i*tye
Don't mention it	**Не за что**
	n*ye*-za-shta
That's OK	**Ничего**
	nichiv*o*
That's good	**Хорошо**
	kharash*o*
I like it	**Мне нравится**
	mnye nr*a*vitsa
That's no good	**Плохо**
	pl*o*kha
I don't like it	**Мне не нравится**
	mnye ni nr*a*vitsa
I know	**(Я) знаю**
	(Y*a*) zn*a*yu
I don't know	**(Я) не знаю**
	(Y*a*) ni zn*a*yu
It doesn't matter	**Неважно**
	niv*a*zhna
Where's the toilet, please?	**Скажите, пожалуйста, где туалет?**
	skazh*i*tye pazh*a*lusta gdye tual*ye*t?
How much is it? [point]	**Сколько это стоит?**
	sk*o*l'ka *e*ta st*o*it
Do you speak English?	**Вы говорите по-английски?**
	vy gavar*i*tye pa-angl*i*ski
I'm sorry ...	**Извините ...**
	izvin*i*tye
I don't speak Russian	**Я не говорю по-русски**
	ya ni gavar'*u* pa-r*u*ski
I only speak a little Russian	**Я плохо говорю по-русски**
	ya pl*o*kha gavar'*u* pa-r*u*ski
I don't understand	**Я не понимаю**
	ya ni panim*a*yu
Please, can you ...	**Будьте добры ...**
	but'tye dabr*y*
repeat this?	**повторите, пожалуйста**
	paftar*i*tye pazh*a*lusta
speak more slowly?	**говорите помедленнее**
	gavar*i*tye pam*ye*dliniye

write it down?	**напишите (это), пожалуйста**
	napishítye (eta) pazhalusta
What is this called in Russian?	**Как это называется по-русски?**
	kak eta nazyvaitsa pa-ruski

Crossing the border

ESSENTIAL INFORMATION

- Look for these signs:
  ТАМОЖНЯ (customs)
  ГРАНИЦА (border)
  [*For further signs and notices, see p. 107*]
- It can take some time to go through the passport control. The official will ask you for your passport and visa which comes as a separate piece of paper.
- There is always an English-speaking official who could help you if there are any problems.
- Before you go through the customs you will be requested to fill in a customs declaration – in English. It is advisable to keep the receipts for things you buy in the hard currency shops called **БЕРЕЗКА,** as you might need them as you go through the customs on the way back.
- You may be asked routine questions by the customs officials [*see below*]. If you have to give personal details see 'Meeting people'. The other important answer to know is 'Nothing': **Ничего** (nichivo).

ROUTINE QUESTIONS

Passport?	**Паспорт?**
	paspart
Where have you come from?	**Откуда Вы приехали?**
	atkuda vy priyekhali
Is this your luggage?	**Это Ваши вещи?**
	eta vashi vyeshi
Open it, please	**Откройте, пожалуйста**
	atkroitye pazhalusta

Meeting people

[*See also 'Everyday expressions', p. 13*]

Breaking the ice

Hello	**Здравствуйте** zdrastvuitye
Good morning	**Доброе утро** dobraye utra
How are you?	**Как Ваши дела?** kak vashi dila
Pleased to meet you	**Очень приятно** ochin' priyatna
I am here ...	**Я здесь** ya zdyes'
on holiday	**отдыхаю** addykhayu
on business	**по делам** pa dilam
Can I offer you ...	**Хотите** khatitye
a drink?	**что-нибудь выпить?** shto-nibut' vypit'
a cigarette?	**сигарету?** sigaryetu
a cigar?	**сигару?** sigaru
Are you staying long?	**Вы надолго приехали?** vy nadolga priyekhali

Name

What's your name?	**Как Вас зовут?** kak vas zavut
My name is ...	**Меня зовут ...** minya zavut

Family

Are you married? (if you ask a woman)	**Вы замужем?** vy zamuzhem
Are you married? (if you ask a man)	**Вы женаты?** vy zhinaty
I am ...	**Я ...** ya ...
married	**замужем / женат** zamuzhem / zhinat
single	**не замужем / неженат** ni-zamuzhem / nizhinat
This is ...	**Это** eta
my wife	**моя жена** maya zhena
my husband	**мой муж** moi muzh
my son	**мой сын** moi syn
my daughter	**моя дочь** maya doch
my (boy) friend	**мой друг** moi druk
my (male) colleague	**мой коллега** moi kalega
my (female) colleague	**моя коллега** maya kalega
Do you have any children?	**У Вас есть дети?** u vas yest' dyeti
I have ...	**У меня есть ...** u minya yest
one daughter	**дочь** doch
one son	**сын** syn
I have ...	**У меня ...** u minya
two daughters	**две дочери** dvye dochiri
two sons	**два сына** dva syna
No, I haven't any children	**У меня нет детей** u minya nyet ditei

Where you live

Are you Russian?	**Вы русский / русская?**
	vy ruskii / ruskaya
I am ...	**Я ...**
	ya
American	**американец / американка**
	amirikanets / amirikanka
English	**англичанин / англичанка**
	anglichanin / anglichanka

[*For other nationalities, see p. 118*]

Where are you from?

I am ...	**Я ...**
	ya iz
from London	**из Лондона**
	londana
from England	**из Англии**
	anglii
from the north	**с севера**
	s-syevira
from the south	**с юга**
	s-yuga
from the east	**с востока**
	s-vastoka
from the west	**с запада**
	z-zapada
from the centre	**из центра**
	is tsentra

[*For other countries, see p. 118*]

For the businessman and woman

I'm from ... (firm's name)	**Я из ...**
	ya iz ...
I have an appointment with ...	**У меня назначена встреча с ...**
	u minya naznachina fstryecha s
May I speak to ...	**Я хотел(а) бы поговорить с ...**
	ya khatyel(a) by pagavarit' s ...
This is my card	**Вот моя карточка**
	vot maya kartachka
I'm sorry I'm late	**Извините за опоздание**
	izvinitye za apazdan'ye
Can I fix another appointment?	**Можно назначить другую встречу?**
	mozhna naznachit' druguyu fstryechu?
I'm staying at the hotel (Moscow)	**Я живу в гостинице (Москва)**
	ya zhivu v-gastinitse (maskva)
I'm staying in N street	**Я живу на улице Н**
	ya zhivu na ulitse N

Asking the way

WHAT TO SAY

Excuse me, please	**Скажите, пожалуйста ...**
	skazhitye, pazhalsta ...
How do I get ...	**Как добраться ...**
	kak dabratsa ...
to Moscow?	**до Москвы**
	da maskvy
to Gorky Street?	**до улицы Горького**
	da ulitsy gor'kava
to the Hotel Metropol?	**до гостиницы Метрополь**
	da gastinitsy mitrapol'
to the airport?	**до аэропорта**
	da airaporta
to the beach?	**до пляжа**
	da plyazha
to the bus station	**до автовокзала**
	da-aftavagzala
to the historic site?	**до старой части города**
	da starai chasti gorada
to the market?	**до рынка**
	da rynka
to the police station?	**до отделения милиции**
	da-addilyeniya militsii
to the port?	**до порта**
	da porta
to the post office?	**до почты**
	da pochty
to the railway?	**до вокзала**
	da vagzala
to the sports stadium?	**до стадиона**
	da stadiona
to the town centre?	**до центра города**
	da tsentra gorada
Excuse me, please ...	**Скажите, пожалуйста ...**
	skazhitye pazhalsta

Is there ... nearby?　　　Где здесь поблизости ...?
　　　　　　　　　　　　　　gdye zdyes' pablizesti ... ?

an art gallery　　　**картинная галерея**
　　　　　　　　　kartinnaya galireya

a baker's　　　**булочная**
　　　　　　bulachnaya

a bank　　　**банк**
　　　　　bank

a bar　　　**бар**
　　　　bar

a botanical garden　　　**ботанический сад**
　　　　　　　　　　batanichiskii sat

a bus stop　　　**остановка автобуса**
　　　　　　astanofka aftobusa

a butcher's　　　**мясной магазин**
　　　　　　misnoi magazin

a café　　　**кафе**
　　　　　kafe

a cake shop　　　**кондитерская**
　　　　　　kanditirskaya

a campsite　　　**кемпинг**
　　　　　kempink

a car park　　　**стоянка автомобилей**
　　　　　　stayanka aftamabilei

a change bureau　　　**бюро обмена валюты**
　　　　　　　byuro abmyena valyuty

a chemist's　　　**аптека**
　　　　　aptyeka

a church　　　**церковь**
　　　　　tserkef'

a cinema　　　**кинотеатр**
　　　　　kinatiatr

a concert hall　　　**концертный зал**
　　　　　　cantsertnyi zal

a delicatessen　　　**кулинария**
　　　　　　kulinariya

a dentist's　　　**зубной врач**
　　　　　zubnoi vrach

a department store　　　**универмаг**
　　　　　　　univirmag

a disco　　　**дискотека**
　　　　diskatyeka

a doctor's surgery	**поликлиника**
	paliklínika
a dry cleaner's	**химчистка**
	khimchístka
a fishmonger's	**рыбный магазин**
	rybnyi magazín
a garage (for repairs)	**станция обслуживания**
	stantsiya apsluzhivan'ya
a hairdresser's	**парикмахерская**
	parikhmakhirskaya
a greengrocer's	**овощной магазин**
	avashnoi magazín
a grocer's	**гастроном**
	gastranom
a hardware shop	**хозяйственный магазин**
	khazyaistvinnyi magazín
a hospital	**больница**
	bal'nítsa
a hotel	**гостиница**
	gastínitsa
a laundry	**прачечная**
	prachichnaya
a museum	**музей**
	muzei
a newsagent's	**газетный киоск**
	gazyetnyi kiosk
a nightclub	**ночной клуб**
	nachnoi klup
a petrol station	**автозаправочная станция**
	afta-zapravachnaya stantsiya
a postbox	**почтовый ящик**
	pachtovyi yashik
a toilet	**туалет**
	tualyet
a restaurant	**ресторан**
	ristaran
a snack bar	**закусочная**
	zakusachnaya
a sports ground	**спортивная площадка**
	spartívnaya plashatka
a supermarket	**гастроном**
	gastranom

a sweet shop	**кондитерская**
	kanditirskaya
a swimming pool	**бассейн**
	basein
a taxi stand	**стоянка такси**
	stayanka taksi
a public telephone	**телефон-автомат**
	tilifon aftamat
a theatre	**театр**
	tiatr
a tobacconist's kiosk	**табачный киоск**
	tabachnyi kiosk
a zoo	**зоопарк**
	zaapark

DIRECTIONS

Left	**Налево**
	Nalyeva
Right	**Направо**
	naprava
Straight on	**Прямо**
	pryama
There	**Там**
	tam
First left/ right	**Первый поворот налево/ направо**
	pyervyi pavarot nalyeva/ naprava
Second left/right	**Второй поворот налево/ направо**
	ftaroi pavarot nalyeva/ naprava
At the crossroads	**На перекрестке**
	na pirikryostkye
At the traffic lights	**У светофора**
	u svitafora
At the level-crossing	**У шлагбаума**
	u shlagbauma

It's near/ far	**Это близко/ далеко**
	eta bliska/daliko
One kilometre	**Один километр**
	adin kilamyetr
Two kilometres	**Два километра**
	dva kilamyetra
Five minutes ...	**Пять минут ...**
	pyat' minut
on foot	**пешком**
	pishkom
by car	**на машине**
	na mashinye
Take ...	**Поезжайте ...**
	paizzhaitye
the bus	**на автобусе**
	na-aftobusye
the train	**на поезде**
	na poizdye
the trolley-bus	**на троллейбусе**
	na traleibusye
the tram	**на трамвае**
	na tramvaye
the underground	**на метро**
	na mitro

[*For public transport, see p. 97*]

The tourist information office

ESSENTIAL INFORMATION

- Every hotel should normally have a tourist information desk.
- There are also information places in town. They look like little kiosks and have a sign **СПРАВКИ.**
- You might have to pay for certain services.
- For finding a tourist office, see p. 21

WHAT TO SAY

Please have you got ...	**Будьте добры, у вас есть ...** but'tye dabry, u vas yest' ...
a plan of the town?	**план города** plan gorada
a list of hotels?	**список гостиниц** spisek gastinits
a list of campsites?	**список кемпингов** spisek kempingef
a list of restaurants?	**список ресторанов** spisek restaranaf
a list of coach excursions?	**список автобусных экскурсий** spisek aftobusnykh ixkursii
a list of events?	**список мероприятий** spisek myerapriyatii
a leaflet on the town?	**брошюра о городе** brashura a goradye
a leaflet on the region?	**брошюра об области** brashura ab oblasti
a railway timetable?	**расписание поездов** raspisan'ye paizdof
a bus timetable?	**расписание автобусов** raspisan'ye aftobusaf
In English, please	**По-английски, пожалуйста** pa-angliski pazhalusta
How much do I owe you?	**Сколько с меня?** skol'ka s-minya

Can you recommend ...	**Посоветуйте, пожалуйста**
	pasav*y*etuitye pazh*a*lusta
a cheap restaurant?	**недорогой ресторан**
	nidarag*oi* ristar*a*n
Can you book a room/ a table for me?	**Вы не могли бы заказать мне номер/ столик?**
	vy ni magl*i* by zakaz*a*t' mnye n*o*mir/st*o*lik

LIKELY ANSWERS

No	**Нет**
	nyet
I'm sorry	**К сожалению**
	k-sazhal*y*en'yu
I don't have a list of campsites	**У нас нет списка кемпингов**
	u nas nyet sp*i*ska k*e*mpingef
It's free	**Это бесплатно**
	*e*ta bispl*a*tna

Accommodation

Hotel

ESSENTIAL INFORMATION

- If you travel to the Soviet Union as a tourist, you have to book your hotel when you book the flight, otherwise no visa will be issued. The best, and cheapest, way is to go with a package tour, which includes the flight, hotel and full board.
- What you get for breakfast varies depending on what is currently available, but would normally include bread, butter, possibly eggs, cheese, cottage cheese, jam, coffee or tea.
- Your guide will take your passport when you arrive and the hotel administration will look after it during your stay. You will be issued with a pass, called **ПРОПУСК** (prОpusk) which you are supposed to have on you when you enter the hotel.
- The guide will normally speak English and should be able to help you should you have any requests or complaints. It is wise to remember, however, that once you have booked your accommodation it would be difficult to change it. There aren't enough hotels in the USSR to accommodate all the people who want to visit the country, and they are normally heavily booked.

WHAT TO SAY

I have a booking	**На мое имя заказан номер**
	na mayo imya zakazan nomir
It's for one person	**Номер на одного**
	nomir na adnavo
two people	**на двоих**
	na dvaikh

[*For numbers, see p. 109*]

It's for one night	**на сутки**
	na sutki
two nights	**на двое суток**
	na dvoye sutak
one week	**на неделю**
	na nidyelyu
two weeks	**на две недели**
	na dvye nidyeli

I would like ...	**Я бы хотел (а) ...**
	ya by khatyel(a) ...
a quiet room	**тихий номер**
	tikhii nomir
two rooms	**два номера**
	dva nomira
with a bathroom	**номер с ванной**
	nomir s-vannai
with a shower	**номер с душем**
	nomir z-dushem
with a cot	**номер с детской кроватью**
	nomir z-dyetskai kravat'yu

At what time is ...	**Когда ...**
	kagda
breakfast/	**завтрак**
	zaftrak
lunch?	**обед**
	abyet
dinner?	**ужин**
	uzhin
How much is it?	**Сколько это стоит?**
	skol'ka eta stoit
Can I look at the room?	**Можно посмотреть номер?**
	mozhna pasmatryet' nomir

Could I have another room?	**Можно поменять номер?**
	mozhna paminyat' nomir
The key to number (ten), please	**Ключ от номера десять, пожалуйста**
	klyuch at nomira dyesit, pazhalusta
Please, may I have ...	**Будьте добры, можно ...**
	buttye dabry mozhna
a coat hanger?	**вешалку**
	vyeshelku
a towel?	**полотенце**
	palatyentse
a glass?	**стакан**
	stakan
some soap?	**мыло**
	myla
an ashtray?	**пепельницу**
	pyepil'nitsu
another pillow?	**еще одну подушку**
	yeshyo adnu padushku
another blanket?	**еще одно одеяло**
	yeshyo adno adiyala
Come in!	**Войдите**
	vaiditye
One moment, please!	**Минуточку!**
	minutechku
Please can you ...	**Будьте добры ...**
	buttye dabry
do this laundry/dry cleaning?	**постирайте/ почистите это**
	pastiraitye/pachistitye eta
call me at ...?	**разбудите меня в ...**
	razbuditye minya v
help me with my luggage?	**помогите мне с багажом**
	pamaghitye mnye z-bagazhom
call me a taxi for ...?	**закажите мне такси на ...**
	zakazhitye mnye taxi na
The bill, please	**Счет, пожалуйста**
	shyot pazhalusta
I think this is wrong	**Мне кажется, это неправильно**
	mnye kazhitsa eta nipravil'na

May I have a receipt?	**Можно квитанцию, пожалуйста**
	mozhna kvitantsiyu pazhalusta

At breakfast

Some more ... please	**Можно еще ... пожалуйста**
	mozhna ishyo pazhalusta
coffee	**кофе**
	kofye
tea	**чаю**
	chayu
bread	**хлеба**
	khlyeba
butter	**масла**
	masla
jam	**варенья**
	varyen'ya
May I have a boiled egg?	**Можно вареное яйцо?**
	mozhna varyonaye yiitso

LIKELY REACTIONS

Have you an identity document, please?	**Пропуск, пожалуйста**
	propusk pazhalusta
What's your name?	**Ваша фамилия?**
	vasha familiya
Sorry, we're full	**К сожалению, свободных номеров нет**
	k-sazhilyen'yu svabodnykh namirof nyet
Do you want to have a look?	**Хотите посмотреть?**
	khatitye pasmatryet'
How many people is it for?	**Сколько вас?**
	skol'ka vas
It's (two) roubles	**Два рубля**
	dva rublya

Camping

ESSENTIAL INFORMATION

- You have to settle your itinerary with the Intourist before going otherwise no visa will be issued.
- Camping facilities in the USSR are very basic. Once again, you are strongly advised to take all the essentials with you, as there are shortages of food and other goods in many parts of the country.
- Once your itinerary has been fixed it is wise to stick to it. The police normally keep a close eye on foreign travellers which means that if you deviate they will soon spot you. So if you are planning a picnic it is best to give them an advance warning.
- Payment for camping facilities is in Intourist coupons.
- Most campsites are only open in the summer.

[*For car travel, see p. 91*]

WHAT TO SAY

Can I pitch a tent here?	**Можно здесь поставить палатку?**
	mozhna zdyes' pastavit' palatku
Where is the nearest camping site?	**Где здесь кемпинг?**
	gdye zdyes' kempink
Have you any vacancies?	**У вас есть свободные места?**
	u-vas yest' svabodnyi mista
How much is it ...	**Сколько стоит ...?**
	skol'ka stoit
for the tent?	**палатка**
	palatka
per day	**В день**
	v-dyen'
Where is ...	**Где ...**
	gdye
the shop?	**магазин**
	magazin

the shower?	душ
	dush
the kitchen?	кухня
	kukhnya
the toilet?	туалет
	tualyet
Where can we eat?	Где здесь можно поесть?
	gdye zdyes' mozhna payest'
Where is the laundry?	Где здесь можно постирать?
	gdye zdyes' mozhna pastirat'
Please, have you got ...	**Скажите, у вас есть ...**
	skazhitye u vas yest'
a broom?	веник? (метла?)
	vyenik (mitla)
a corkscrew?	штопор
	shtopar
a drying-up cloth?	тряпка
	tryapka
a fork?	вилка
	vilka
a fridge?	холодильник
	khaladil'nik
a frying pan?	сковородка?
	skavarotka
an iron?	утюг
	utyuk
a knife?	нож
	nosh
a plate?	тарелка
	taryelka
a saucepan?	кастрюля
	kastryulya
a teaspoon?	чайная ложка
	chainaya loshka
a tin opener?	открывалка
	atkryvalka
any washing powder?	стиральный порошок
	stiral'nyi parashok
How much do I owe you?	Сколько с меня?
	skol'ka s-minya

Problems

The toilet	**Туалет**
	tual*yet*
The shower	**Душ**
	dush
The tap	**Кран**
	kran
The light	**Свет**
	svyet
... is not working	**не работает**
	ni rabotait
My camping gas has run out	**У меня кончился газ**
	u min*ya* k*o*nchilsya gas

LIKELY REACTIONS

Your documents, please	**Ваши документы**
	vashi dakum*yenty*
What's your name?	**Ваша фамилия?**
	vasha fam*i*liya
Sorry, we're full	**Мест нет**
	myest nyet
It's (10) coupons	**С вас (10) купонов**
	s-vas d*ye*syat' kup*o*naf

General shopping

All sorts of things are in short supply in the Soviet Union, so it is strongly advisable to take all the essentials with you. If there are any items you cannot do without, take a reasonable supply. Do not rely on being able to get them there. This would include all the toiletries.

The chemist's

ESSENTIAL INFORMATION

- Look for the word **АПТЕКА** (chemist's).
- Medicines are available only at a chemist's.
- Chemists are normally open until 8p.m., but there are some which stay open throughout the night. Ask for **ДЕЖУРНАЯ АПТЕКА** (dizhurnaya aptyeka) if you need the chemist's late at night.
- It is strongly advisable to take basic medicaments and toiletries with you as it is hard to rely on the availability of such things in the USSR.
- There is normally a medical room at the hotel, and if you are feeling ill, the hotel staff will call a doctor for you.

WHAT TO SAY

Have you got (any) ...	**У вас есть ...?** u vas yest'
antiseptic	**дезинфицирующее средство** dizinfitsiruyusheye sretstva
aspirin	**аспирин** aspirin
bandage	**бинт** bint
cotton wool	**вата** vata
eye drops	**глазные капли** glaznyye kapli
insect repellent	**средство от насекомых** sryetstva at nasikomykh
lip salve	**крем для губ** krem dlya gup
sticking plaster	**пластырь** plastyr'
Vaseline	**вазелин** vazilin
soap	**мыло** myla
shaving cream	**крем для бритья** krem dlya brit'ya
handcream	**крем для рук** krem dlya ruk
toothpaste	**зубная паста** zubnaya pasta
some suntan lotion	**крем для загара** krem dlya zagara

Have you got anything for ...	**У вас есть что-нибудь от ...**
	u vas yest' shtonibut' at
bites	**укусов**
	ukusaf
burns	**ожогов**
	azhogaf
chilblains	**обмораживания**
	abmarazhivaniya
a cold	**простуды**
	prastudy
constipation	**запора**
	zapora
a cough	**кашля**
	kashlya
diarrhoea	**поноса**
	panosa
flu	**гриппа**
	gripa

[*For other essential expressions, see 'Shop talk', p. 48*]

Holiday items

ESSENTIAL INFORMATION

- Places to shop and signs to look for:
  КНИГИ (bookshop)
  УНИВЕРМАГ (department store)

WHAT TO SAY

Where can I buy ... ?	**Где можно купить ...**
	gdye mozhna kupit'
Have you got ... ?	**У вас есть ...**
	u vas yest'
a bag	**сумка**
	sumka
a beach ball	**мяч**
	myach
a bucket	**ведерко**
	vidyorka
English newspapers	**английские газеты**
	angliskiye gazyety
some envelopes	**конверты**
	kanvyerty
a guide book	**путеводитель**
	putivaditil'
a map (of the area)	**карта (области)**
	karta oblasti
some postcards	**открытки**
	atkrytki
a spade	**лопатка**
	lapatka
a straw hat	**соломенная шляпа**
	salominaya shlyapa
a suitcase	**чемодан**
	chimadan
some sunglasses	**темные очки**
	tyomnyi achki
a sunshade	**козырек**
	kazyryok

an umbrella	**зонтик**
	zontik
some writing paper	**бумага для писем**
	bumaga dlya pisim
a colour film	**цветная пленка**
	tsvitnaya plyonka
a black-and-white film	**черно-белая пленка**
	chyorna-byelaya plyonka
for prints	**для фотографий**
	dlya fatagrafii
for slides	**для слайдов**
	dlya slaidaf
This camera is broken	**У меня не работает аппарат**
	u-minya ni rabotait aparat
Please can you ...	**Будьте добры ...**
	but'tye dabry
develop/print this?	**проявите это**
	prayavitye eta

[For other essential expressions, see 'Shop talk', p. 48]

The tobacconist's

ESSENTIAL INFORMATION

● Tobacco is sold in kiosks called **ТАБАК**.

WHAT TO SAY

A packet of cigarettes ...	**Пачку сигарет, пожалуйста ...** pachku sigaryet pazhalusta
with filters	**с фильтром** s-fil'tram
without filters	**без фильтра** bis-fil'tra
Those up there ...	**Вот этих** vot etikh
on the right	**справа** sprava
on the left	**слева** slyeva
These [*point*]	**Эти** eti
Two packets	**Две пачки** dvye pachki
Have you got ...	**У вас есть ...** u vas yest'
English cigarettes?	**английские сигареты** angliskiye sigaryety
American cigarettes	**американские сигареты** amirikanskiye sigaryety
English pipe tobacco	**английский трубочный табак** angliskii trubachnyi tabak
American pipe tobacco	**американский трубочный табак** amirikanskii trubachnyi tabak
A packet of pipe tobacco	**Пачку табака пожалуйста** pachku tabaka pazhalusta

That one up there ...	**Вот того ...**
	vot-tav*o*
on the right	**справа**
	spr*a*va
on the left	**слева**
	sl*ye*va
This one [*point*]	**Вот этот**
	vot-*e*tat
A cigar, please	**Сигару, пожалуйста**
	sig*a*ru pazh*a*lusta
A packet of cigars, please	**Пачку сигар, пожалуйста**
	p*a*chku sig*a*r pazh*a*lusta
Those [*point*]	**Вот эти**
	vot *e*ti
A box of matches	**Спички, пожалуйста**
	sp*i*chki pazh*a*lusta

[*For other essential expressions, see 'Shop talk', p. 48*]

Buying clothes

ESSENTIAL INFORMATION

- Look for:
  ОДЕЖДА (clothes)
  ОБУВЬ (shoes)
- Don't buy without trying things on first.
- Don't rely on conversion charts of clothing sizes [*see p. 124*].
- If you are buying for someone else, take their measurements with you.

WHAT TO SAY

If you want to buy gifts you can do it at the special shops for foreigners. They are called **БЕРЁЗКА** (BERYOZKA) and you pay there in hard currency. They are normally better stocked than the ordinary Soviet shops.

You can, however, try and do some shopping at an ordinary shop where you can only pay in roubles.

First of all you have to attract the attention of the shop assistant. Practically all of them are women, so the thing to say is:

ДЕВУШКА dyevushka.

Then it is best to ask if the item you need is available:

Have you got ... ?	**У вас есть ...?**
	u vas yest'
Could you show me ...	**Покажите, пожалуйста**
	pakazhitye pazhalusta
this belt	**этот пояс**
	etat pois
this coat	**это пальто**
	eta pal'to

May I have a look at ...?	**Можно посмотреть ...?**
	mozhna pasmatryet'
this dress	**это платье**
	eta plat'ye
these gloves	**эти перчатки**
	eti pirchatki
this hat	**эту шляпу**
	etu shlyapu
this fur hat	**эту шапку**
	etu shapku
these mittens	**эти варежки**
	eti varishki
this shirt	**эту рубашку**
	etu rubashku
these shoes	**эти туфли**
	eti tufli
these socks	**эти носки**
	eti naski
this T-shirt	**эту майку**
	etu maiku
Can I try it on?	**Можно померять?**
	mozhna pamyerit'

[*For other essential expressions, see 'Shop talk', p. 48*]

Replacing equipment

ESSENTIAL INFORMATION

- Look for these shops and signs:
  ХОЗЯЙСТВЕННЫЙ МАГАЗИН (hardware)
  ЭДЕКТРОТОВАРЫ (electrical goods)
- To ask the way to the shop, see p. 21.

WHAT TO SAY

Have you got ...	**У вас есть ...**
	u vas yest'
a bottle of butane gas?	**газовые баллоны**
	gazavye balony
a bottle opener?	**открывалка**
	atkryvalka
a corkscrew?	**штопор**
	shtopar
any disinfectant?	**дезинфицирующие средства**
	dizinfitsiruyushiye sryetstva
a drying-up cloth?	**тряпка**
	tryapka
any forks?	**вилки**
	vilki
a fuse? (show old one)	**пробка**
	propka
an insecticide spray?	**средство от насекомых**
	sryetstva at nasikomykh
any knives?	**ножи**
	nazhi
a light bulb (show old one)	**лампочка**
	lampachka
a plastic bucket?	**пластмассовое ведро**
	plasmassavaye vidro
a scouring pad?	**мочалка для посуды**
	machalka dlya pasudy
a spanner?	**гаечный ключ**
	gaichnyi klyuch
a sponge?	**губка**
	gupka

any string?	**веревка**
	viryofka
a tin opener?	**открывалка**
	atkryvalka
a torch?	**фонарь**
	fanar'
any torch batteries?	**батарейки для фонаря**
	batareiki dlya fanarya
a plug? (for the sink)	**затычка**
	zatychka
any washing powder?	**стиральный порошок**
	stiral'nyi parashok

Shop talk

ESSENTIAL INFORMATION

- Know your coins and notes
  coins: see illustration overleaf
  notes: 1 rouble, 3 roubles, 5 roubles, 10 roubles, 25 roubles, 50 roubles.
- Know how to say the important weights and measures:

50 grams	**пятьдесят граммов**
	piddis*y*at gram
100 grams	**сто граммов**
	sto gram
200 grams	**двести граммов**
	dv*y*esti gram
½ kilo	**полкило**
	polkil*o*
1 kilo	**килограмм**
	kilagram
2 kilos	**два килограмма**
	dva kilagr*a*ma
½ litre	**поллитра**
	pol-l*i*tra
1 litre	**литр**
	litr
2 litre	**два литра**
	dva l*i*tra

[*For numbers, see p. 109*]

- Bargaining is not customary in shops, but sometimes works in the market. Remember that market prices are steep and everything costs much more than in the shops. However, markets are often the only places where you would be able to obtain fresh fruit and vegetables.
- Unfortunately, shop assistants are often not particularly helpful. Don't pay attention to that and insist on being served. As most of them are women, the best way to attract their attention is to say **ДЕВУШКА** (d*y*evushka).

CUSTOMER

Hello	**Здравствуйте** zdrastvuitye
Good morning	**Доброе утро** dobraye utra
Good day	**Добрый день**
Good afternoon	dobryi dyen'
Good evening	**Добрый вечер** dobryi vyechir
Goodbye	**До свидания** da-svidan'ya
I'm just looking	**Я просто смотрю** ya prosta smatryu
Excuse me	**Простите** prastitye
How much is this/that?	**Сколько это стоит?** skol'ka eta stoit
What is that?	**Что это?** shto eta
Could I have a look at this, please	**Можно это посмотреть** mozhna eta pasmatryet'
Could you show me this, please	**Покажите это, пожалуйста** pakazhitye eta pazhalusta
Not that	**Нет, не это** nyet, ni-eta
That's enough, thank you	**Это все, спасибо** eta vsyo spasiba
More, please	**Еще, пожалуйста** yishyo pazhalusta
Less than that, please	**Не так много, пожалуйста** ni tak mnoga pazhalusta
That's fine	**Достаточно, спасибо**
OK	dastatachna, spasiba
I won't take it, thank you	**Я это не возьму, спасибо** ya eta ni-vaz'mu spasiba
It's not right	**Мне это не подходит** mnye eta ni-patkhodit
Thank you very much	**Большое спасибо** bal'shoye spasiba

Have you got something ...	**У вас есть что-нибудь ...**
	u vas yest' shto-nibut'
better?	**получше**
	pal*u*chshye
cheaper?	**подешевле**
	padish*e*vlye
different?	**другое**
	drug*o*ye
larger?	**побольше**
	pab*o*l'she
smaller?	**поменьше**
	pam*y*en'she
At what time does the shop ...	**В котором часу магазин ...**
	f-kat*o*ram chis*u* magaz*i*n
open?	**открывается**
	atkryv*a*itsa
close?	**закрывается**
	zakryv*a*itsa
Can I have a receipt?	**Дайте, пожалуйста, чек**
	d*a*itye pazh*a*lusta chek
Do you take ...	**Вы берете ...**
	vy bir*y*otye
English/American money?	**английскую/ американскую валюту**
	angl*i*skuyu/ amirik*a*nskuyu val*yu*tu
travellers' cheques?	**чеки**
	ch*y*eki
credit cards?	**кредитные карточки**
	krid*i*tnyi k*a*rtachki
I'd like that ...	**Дайте, пожалуйста, это ...**
	d*a*itye pazh*a*lusta *e*ta

SHOP ASSISTANT

Can I help you?	**Я Вас слушаю**
	ya vas slushiyu
What would you like?	**Что Вы хотите?**
	shto vy khatitye
Will that be all?	**Это все?**
Is that all?	eta fsyo
Would you like it wrapped?	**Вам завернуть?**
	vam zavirnut'
Sorry, none left	**К сожалению, продано**
	k-sazhalyen'u prodana
I haven't got any	**Нет**
	nyet
I haven't got any more	**Больше нет**
	bol'she nyet
How many do you want?	**Сколько вам?**
How much do you want?	skol'ka vam
Is that enough?	**Достаточно?**
	dastatachna

Shopping for food

Bread

ESSENTIAL INFORMATION

- Key words to look for:
  БУЛОЧНАЯ (baker's)
  ХЛЕБ (bread)
- For finding a baker's, see p. 22.
- Most supermarkets sell bread.
- Most shops selling food are open seven days a week from 8a.m.
  to 1p.m. and from 2p.m. to 9p.m., closing at lunch time. It is
  not uncommon for the doors to shut 10 to 15 minutes before
  official closing time.
- All bread is sold by item, with larger loaves normally being cut
  into halves or quarters.
- Bakeries also often sell sweets, either already packed, or at a
  special counter.

WHAT TO SAY

Some bread, please	**Хлеб, пожалуйста** khlyep pazhalusta
A white loaf	**Батон белого** baton byelava
A brown loaf	**Буханку черного** bukhanku chornava
Half a loaf	**Полбуханки** pol-bukhanki
A quarter of a loaf	**четвертинку** chitvirtinku
A bread roll	**Булочку** bulychku
Four bread rolls	**четыре булочки** chityri bulychki
A bun	**булочка** bulychka

Cakes and sweets

ESSENTIAL INFORMATION

- Key words to look for:
  БУЛОЧНАЯ-КОНДИТЕРСКАЯ (bakery and patisserie)
  КУЛИНАРИЯ (delicatessen)
  КАФЕТЕРИЙ (a place to have a bun or cake and tea or coffee).
- To find a cake shop etc., see p. 22.
- To order a snack, see p. 71.

WHAT TO SAY

The types of cake you find in the shops vary enormously from region to region, but the following are some of the most common.

Торт tort	gateau
Кекс kyeks	a kind of fruit cake
Рулет roulyet	a swiss roll
Пирожное pirozhnaye	any type of cream cake
Пирог pirok	a pie
Пончик ponchik	a doughnut

Gateaux are normally sold by item, but if you are having a coffee in one of the cafeterias you might need to ask for a piece of cake, in which case you'll have to say:

A piece of cake, please	**Кусок торта, пожалуйста** kousok torta pazhalusta
Two cream cakes	**Два пирожных** dva pirozhnykh

The following you buy mostly by weight although biscuits are also sold by packets:

A packet of biscuits, please	**Пачку печенья, пожалуйста** pachku pichen' ya pazhalusta
200 grams of biscuits	**Двести граммов печенья** dvyesti gram pichyen'ya
½ kilo of gingerbread	**Полкило пряников** polkilo pryanikaf
300 grams of sweets	**Триста граммов конфет** trista gram kanfyet
These/those ones, please	**Вот этих / тех** vot-etikh / tyekh
Marshmallow	**Зефир** zifir
Fruit fudge	**Пастила** pastila
Jelly sweets	**Мармелад** marmilat
Toffees	**Ириски** iriski
Boiled sweets	**Карамель** karamyel'
Lollies	**Леденцы** lidintsy

Ice-cream

ESSENTIAL INFORMATION

- Key word to look for:
  МОРОЖЕНОЕ (ice-cream)
- Ice-cream is probably the only type of fast food you can rely on being always able to get in the USSR. It is usually sold in special kiosks, not in supermarkets.
- The types of ice-cream available are usually displayed in the kiosk window, together with the price, so the thing to do is to name the price of the ice-cream you want. For example:

За пятнадцать, пожалуйста za pitnatsit' pazhalusta	an ice-cream costing 15 kopeks, please
За двадцать две za dvatsit' dvye	an ice-cream costing 22 kopeks

OTHER THINGS TO SAY

A chocolate ice-cream	**шоколадное мороженое** shakaladnaye marozhnoye
A fruit-flavoured ice	**Фруктовое мороженое** fruktovaye marozhnaye
A cream ice	**Сливочное мороженое** slivachnaye marozhnaye
Two ices, please	**Два, пожалуйста** dva pazhalusta

Ice-cream kiosks sometimes also sell bars of chocolate.

A bar of chocolate, please	**Плитку шоколада, пожалуйста** plitku shakalada pazhalusta
Two bars of chocolate	**Две плитки шоколада** dvye plitki shakalada

Other sweets are sold in the bakeries/patisseries.

In the supermarket

ESSENTIAL INFORMATION

- The place to ask for:
  ГАСТРОНОМ (supermarket)
  УНИВЕРСАМ (also a supermarket, a bigger one, but not necessarily better stocked).
- Key instructions on signs in the shop:
  ВХОД (entrance)
  ВЫХОД (exit)
  ВХОДА НЕТ (no entry)
  КАССА (cash desk)
  САМООБЛУЖИВАНИЕ (self-service)
- Opening times are usually 8a.m. to 1p.m. and 2p.m. to 9p.m. (sometimes 8p.m.). Most shops, except a few large department stores, close for lunch.
- For non-food items, Replacing equipment, p. 46.
- No need to say anything in a supermarket, but ask if you can't find what you want.

WHAT TO SAY

Could you tell me where ... is, please?	**Скажите, пожалуйста, где ...?**
	skazhitye pazhalusta gdye
the bread	**хлеб**
	khlyep
the butter	**масло**
	masla
the cheese	**сыр**
	syr
the chocolate	**шоколад**
	shakalat
the coffee	**кофе**
	kofe
the cooking oil	**растительное масло**
	rastitil'naye masla
the fish	**рыба**
	ryba
the fruit	**фрукты**
	froukty
the honey	**мед**
	myot
the jam	**варенье**
	varyen'ye
the meat	**мясо**
	myasa
the milk	**молоко**
	malako
the mineral water	**минеральная вода**
	miniral'naya vada
the salt	**соль**
	sol'
the sugar	**сахар**
	sakhar
the tea	**чай**
	chai
the tinned fish	**рыбные консервы**
	rybnyi kansyervy
the tinned fruit	**консервированные фрукты**
	kansirviravanyi froukty

the vinegar	**уксус**
	uksus
the wine	**вино**
	vino
the yoghurt	**кефир**
	kifir
the biscuits	**печенье**
	pichyen'ye
the eggs	**яйца**
	yaitsa
the fruit juices	**соки**
	soki
the pastas	**макароны**
	makarony
the vegetables	**овощи**
	ovashi

[*For other essential expressions, see 'Shop talk', p. 48*]

Fruit and vegetables

ESSENTIAL INFORMATION

- Key words to look for:
  ФРУКТЫ (fruit)
  ОВОЩИ (vegetables)
- In the state shops and supermarkets fruit and vegetables are practically always in short supply, even the most basic ones, and there isn't a great deal of choice, except in autumn. Markets offer more variety, but prices there are often prohibitive. If you are a vegetarian you might find life in this respect a little dull and difficult.
- When you shop (whether in a supermarket or market) you must take your own shopping bag – paper bags are not usually provided, and plastic bags (if available) are expensive and not particularly reliable.

WHAT TO SAY

½ kilo of ...	**полкило ...**
	pol-kilo
1 kilo of ...	**килограмм ...**
	kilagram
2 kilos of ...	**два килограмма ...**
	dva kilagrama
apples	**яблок**
	yablak
apricots	**абрикосов**
	abrikosaf
bananas	**бананов**
	bananaf
cherries	**вишен**
	vishin
figs (dried)	**фиников**
	finikaf
grapes	**винограда**
	vinagrada
grapefruit	**грейпфрутов**
	greip-frutaf

oranges	**апельсинов**
	apil's*i*naf
peaches	**персиков**
	p*y*ersikaf
pears	**груш**
	groush
plums	**слив**
	slif
strawberries	**клубники**
	kloubn*i*ki
A melon	**дыня**
	dynya
A water-melon	**арбуз**
	arb*us*
½ kilo of ...	**полкило ...**
	pol-kil*o*
A kilo of ...	**килограмм ...**
	kilag*r*am
1½ kilos of ...	**полтора килограмма ...**
	paltar*a* kilagrama
2 kilos of ...	**два килограмма ...**
	dva kilag*r*ama
aubergines	**баклажанов**
	baklazh*a*naf
beetroot	**свеклы**
	sv*y*okly
beans	**фасоли**
	fas*o*li
carrots	**моркови**
	mark*o*vi
mushrooms	**грибов**
	grib*o*f
onions	**лука**
	l*u*ka
peppers	**перцев**
	p*y*ertsef
potatoes	**картошки**
	kart*o*shki
spring onions	**зеленого лука**
	zil*y*onava l*u*ka

tomatoes	**помидоров**
	pamid*o*raf
A bunch of ...	**Пучок ...**
	pouch*o*k
dill	**укропа**
	ukr*o*pa
parsley	**петрушки**
	pitr*u*shki
radishes	**редиски**
	rid*i*ski
salad	**салата**
	sal*a*ta
A head of garlic	**Головку чеснока**
	gal*o*fku chisn*a*ka
A cauliflower	**Кочан цветной капусты**
	kach*a*n tsvitn*oi* kap*u*sty
A cabbage	**Кочан капусты**
	kach*a*n kap*u*sty
A cucumber	**Огурец**
	agur*y*ets
This one, please	**Этот, пожалуйста**
	*e*tat pazh*a*lusta

[*For other essential information, see 'Shop talk', p. 48*]

Meat

ESSENTIAL INFORMATION

- Key words to look for:
  МЯСО (butcher's)
- In the state-run shops meat has been scarce in the USSR for a long time and, when it is available, is of poor quality. There is more choice at the markets, but, as with other foodstuffs, the prices are prohibitive.

[*For numbers, see p. 109*]

WHAT TO SAY

½ kilo of ..., please	**Полкило ... пожалуйста** polkilo ... pazhalusta
beef	**говядины** gavyadiny
lamb	**баранины** baraniny
pork	**свинины** svininy
veal	**телятины** tilyatiny
1 kilo of ...	**Килограмм ...** kilagram
liver	**печени** pyechini
kidneys	**почек** pochik
sausages	**сосисок** sasisak
mince	**фарша** farsha
Two chops, please	**Две отбивных, пожалуйста** dvye, atbivnykh pazhalusta
A chicken, please	**Курицу, пожалуйста** kuritsu pazhalusta
A duck, please	**Утку, пожалуйста** utku pazhalusta

Fish

ESSENTIAL INFORMATION

- Key word to look for:
  РЫБА (fish)
- Markets sometimes have fresh fish stalls.
- Most of the fish sold in the shops is frozen and, as with meat, there is very little variety. However, in some places near the sea (the Baltic states, for example) the situation might be a little better.
- There are various types of tinned fish, but it is not always very fresh. Sell-by dates are often not marked on the foodstuffs. It is not customary for the shop assistants to clean the fish, take the heads off or fillet it.

  One type of fish that is very popular throughout Russia is herring, salted or pickled. It is called:

  Селедка   herring
  sil*yo*tka

WHAT TO SAY

Cod	**Треска** trisk*a*
Lobster	**Рак** rak
Plaice	**Камбала** k*a*mbala
Prawns	**Креветки** krivy*e*tki
Red mullet	**Окунь** *o*kun'
Sardines	**Сардины** sard*i*ny
Sturgeon	**Осетрина/ севрюга** asitr*i*na/ sivr*y*uga

A tin of ... please	**Банку ... пожалуйста**
	banku ... pazhalusta
caviar	**икры**
	ikry
sardines	**сардин**
	sardin
sprats	**шпрот**
	shprot

Eating and drinking out

Ordering a drink

ESSENTIAL INFORMATION

- Key words to look for:
- **КАФЕТЕРИЙ** (a snack bar)
  КАФЕ (a café)
  БАР (a bar)
  КАФЕ-МОРОЖЕНОЕ (a café which serves mainly ice-creams and coffee)
  ПИВНОЙ БАР (beer bar – not at all like a pub. Can be grubby)
- Opening hours vary depending on the establishment and can be very erratic. Some close for an hour after lunch and reopen at 4 or 5p.m.
- Children are allowed in.
- The new cooperative cafés are private enterprises and often offer a better choice and service. They are however more expensive.
- Tea is never served with milk, so if you ask for it, you might get a cup of tea and a glass of milk.

WHAT TO SAY

I'll have ... please	Будьте добры ...
	but'tye dabry
a cocoa	**какао**
	cacao
a black coffee	**черный кофе**
	chornyi kofe
a coffee with milk	**кофе с молоком**
	kofe s-malakom
tea	**чай**
	chai
tea with lemon	**чай с лимоном**
	chai s-limonam

tea with milk	**чай с молоком**
	chai s-malak*o*m
a glass of milk	**стакан молока**
	stak*a*n malak*a*
a mineral water	**стакан минеральной воды**
	stak*a*n miniral'nai vad*y*
a lemonade	**лимонад**
	liman*a*t
a Pepsi-Cola	**Пепси**
	p*e*psi
an apple juice	**яблочный сок**
	*y*ablachnyi sok
a grape juice	**виноградный сок**
	vinagra*d*nyi sok
a mandarin juice	**мандариновый сок**
	mandar*i*navyi sok
an orange juice	**апельсиновый сок**
	apil's*i*navyi sok
A mug of beer, please	**Кружку пива, пожалуйста**
	kr*u*shku p*i*va pazhalusta
Two mugs of beer	**Две кружки пива**
	dvye kr*u*shki p*i*va
A glass of juice	**Стакан сока**
	stak*a*n s*o*ka
Two glasses of milk	**Два стакана молока**
	dva stak*a*na malak*a*
A bottle of milk	**Бутылку молока**
	but*y*lku malak*a*
Two bottles of ...	**Две бутылки ...**
	dvye but*y*lki
red wine	**красного вина**
	kr*a*snava vin*a*
white wine	**белого вина**
	b*y*elava vin*a*
vodka	**водки**
	v*o*tki
dry	**сухого**
	sukh*o*va
sweet	**сладкого**
	slatkava

champagne	**шампанского** shampanskava
A whisky	**Виски** viski
with ice	**со льдом** sa-l'dom
with water	**с водой** s-vadoi
A gin	**Джин** jin
with tonic	**с тоником** s-tonikam
with lemon	**с лимоном** s-limonam
A brandy	**Коньяк** kan'yak

The local drink you might like to try is:

КВАС kvass	A sweetish drink made of fermented black bread

Other essential expressions:

Miss!	**Девушка!** dyevushka
Waiter!	**Официант!** afitsiant
The bill, please	**Счет, пожалуйста** shyot pazhalusta
How much does that come to?	**Сколько с меня?** skol'ka s-minya
Where is the toilet, please?	**Скажите, пожалуйста, где туалет?** skazhitye pazhalusta gdye tualyet

Ordering a snack

ESSENTIAL INFORMATION

- Look for a café or bar with these signs:
  КАФЕ (a café)
  КАФЕТЕРИЙ (a café)
  СТОЛОВАЯ (a canteen – usually not very good)
  ЗАКУСОЧНАЯ (a snack-bar)
- If you see a sign **КООПЕРАТИВНОЕ КАФЕ** it means that it is a privately run establishment. The food and service tend to be better, but it is also more expensive.

WHAT TO SAY

I'll have ... please	Мне, пожалуйста, ...
	mnye pazhalusta
a caviar sandwich	**Бутерброд с икрой**
	boutyrbrot s-ikroi
a cheese sandwich	**Бутерброд с сыром**
	boutyrbrot s-syram
a ham sandwich	**Бутерброд с ветчиной**
	boutyrbrot s-vitchinoi
a salami sandwich	**Бутерброд с колбасой**
	boutyrbrot s-kalbasoi
a smoked fish sandwich	**Бутерброд с рыбой**
	boutyrbrot s-rybai
a meat pasty	**Пирожок с мясом**
	pirazhok s-myasam
a cabbage pasty	**Пирожок с капустой**
	pirazhok s-kapustai

[*For other essential expressions, see 'Ordering a drink', p. 67*]

In a restaurant

ESSENTIAL INFORMATION

- The sign to look for is:
  РЕСТОРАН (restaurant)
- Some cafés also serve food, and it is probably worth trying a
  КООПЕРАТИВНОЕ КАФЕ
- You will find the names of the principal ingredients of most
  dishes on these pages:

Meat, see p. 63	Fruit, see p. 60
Fish, see p. 64	Dessert, see p. 56
Vegetables, see p. 60	Ice-cream, see p. 56

- Restaurants are quite expensive. Service is usually not in-
  cluded, and it is customary to give a tip to the waiter. How
  much you give is entirely up to you.
- If the restaurant is good you might have to queue for some
  time, so it is best to book in advance.
- If you have a complaint you should ask for a book of complaints. Here is the way to ask for it:
  ДАЙТЕ ПОЖАЛУЙСТА ЖАЛОБНУЮ КНИГУ
  daitye pazhalusta *zh*alabnuyu kn*i*gu
- Restaurants usually open at 6p.m. or 7p.m. and close around
  11p.m., although some might go on until midnight.

WHAT TO SAY

May I book a table?	**Можно заказать столик?**
	m*o*zhna zakaz*a*t' st*o*lik
I've booked a table	**Я заказывал столик**
	ya zak*a*zyval st*o*lik
A table ...	**Столик на ...**
	st*o*lik na
for one	**на одного**
	na-adnav*o*
for two	**на двоих**
	na-dvaikh
for three	**на троих**
	na-tra*i*kh

The menu, please	**Дайте, пожалуйста, меню**
	daitye pazhalusta minu
What's this, please?	**Скажите, пожалуйста, что это?**
	skazhitye pazhalusta shto eta
A bottle of ...	**Бутылку ...**
	butylku
champagne	**шампанского**
	shampanskava
mineral water	**минеральной воды**
	miniral'nai vady
vodka	**водки**
	votki
wine	**вина**
	vina
Red/ white wine	**Красного/ белого вина**
	krasnava/ byelava vina
Dry/ sweet wine	**Сухого/ сладкого вина**
	sukhova/ slatkava vina
Some more wine, please	**Еще вина, пожалуйста**
	yisho vina pazhalusta
Salt	**Соль**
	sol'
Pepper	**Перец**
	pyerits
Some water, please	**Воды, пожалуйста**
	vady pazhalusta
Some more bread, please	**Дайте, пожалуйста, еще хлеба**
	daitye pazhalusta yisho khlyeba
Can I/we have the bill, please	**Счет, пожалуйста**
	shyot pazhalusta
Where is the toilet, please?	**Скажите, пожалуйста, где туалет?**
	skazhitye pazhalusta gdye tualyet
Miss!	**Девушка!**
	dyevushka
Waiter!	**Официант!**
	afitsiant

Key words for courses as seen on some menus

STARTERS	**Закуски** zakuski
SOUPS	**Супы** soupy
FISH	**Рыбные блюда** rybnyi blyuda
MEAT	**Мясные блюда** misnyi blyuda
GAME	**Дичь** dich
FOWL	**Птица** ptitsa
VEGETABLES	**Овощи** ovashi
CHEESE	**Сыр** syr
FRUIT	**Фрукты** froukty
ICE-CREAMS	**Мороженое** marozhnaye
DESSERT	**Дессерт** disyert

Cooking and menu terms

вареный var*y*oni	boiled, poached
тушеный toush*o*nyi	stewed
копченый kapch*o*nyi	smoked
жареный zh*a*rinyi	fried
маринованный marin*o*vanyi	marinated
соленый sal*y*onyi	pickled
запеченый zapich*o*nyi	baked
жаркое zhark*o*ye	pot-roasted
фаршированный farshir*o*vanyi	stuffed

Quite a few restaurants have menus translated into English. Remember that the country is enormous and there is endless variety of traditional dishes depending on the region.
Here, however, are a few words that might help you understand the menu.

грибы в сметане grib*y* f-smit*a*nye	mushrooms in sour cream
борщ borsh	beetroot soup

шашлык shashlyk	shashlik, kebab
блины bliny	pancakes (eaten with savoury filling)
блинчики blinchiki	stuffed pancakes
салат salat	salad
винегрет vinigryet	potato salad with beetroot and pickled cucumbers
паштет pashtyet	pâté
голубцы galubtsy	stuffed cabbage leaves
пельмени pil'myeni	a kind of ravioli
плов plof	pilav
икра из баклажан ikra iz baklazhan	aubergine caviar
уха ukha	fish soup
соус soous	sauce
яичница yiishnitsa	fried eggs
тефтели tiftyeli	meat balls
беф-строганов bef-stroganaf	beef Stroganoff
гречневая каша gryechnivaya kasha	buckwheat porridge
манная каша mannaya kasha	semolina
запеканка zapikanka	a kind of pudding or soufflé
компот kampot	compote

Health

ESSENTIAL INFORMATION

- There are no reciprocal health agreements between the UK and the USSR. It is advisable to arrange medical insurance before you go and make sure that if you might need some medical treatment, you have it before you go.
- Take your own first-aid kit with you.
- If you feel unwell your guide or an administrator at the hotel will call a doctor for you.

WHAT'S THE MATTER?

I have a pain in my ...	У меня болит ... u minya balit
abdomen	живот zhivot
ankle	лодыжка ladyshka
arm	рука rouka
back	спина spina
breast	грудь grout'
ear	ухо oukha
eye	глаз glas
foot	нога naga
head	голова galava
heel	пятка pyatka
jaw	челюсть chyelyust'
leg	нога naga

neck	**шея**
	sheya
shoulder	**плечо**
	plicho
stomach	**желудок**
	zhiloudak
throat	**горло**
	gorla
wrist	**запястье**
	zapyast'ye
I have a pain in my ...	**У меня боли ...**
	u-minya boli
bladder	**в мочевом пузыре**
	v-machivom pouzyrye
bowels	**в кишечнике**
	f-kishechnikye
chest	**в груди**
	v-groudi
groin	**в паху**
	f-pakhu
lung	**в легких**
	v-lyokhkikh
vagina	**в матке**
	v-matkye
I have a pain in my kidney	**У меня болят почки**
	u-minya balyat pochki
I have toothache	**У меня болит зуб**
	u-minya balit zoup
I have broken my glasses	**Я разбил очки**
	ya pazbil achki
My child is ill	**Мой ребенок болен**
	moi ribyonak bolyen
He/she has a pain in his/ her ...	**У него/ у нее болит ...**
	u-nivo/ u-niyo balit
How bad is it?	**Сильно болит?**
	sil'na balit
I'm ill	**Я заболел/ заболела**
	ya zabalyel/ zabalyela
It's urgent	**Это срочно**
	eta srochna

It's serious	**Это серьезно** eta sir'yozna
It's not serious	**Это не серьезно** eta ni-sir'yozna
It hurts	**Больно** bol'na
It hurts a lot	**Очень больно** ochin' bol'na
It doesn't hurt much	**Не очень больно** ni ochin' bol'na
The pain occurs ...	**Боли повторяются ...** boli paftaryayutsa
every quarter of an hour	**каждые четверть часа** kazhdyi chyetvirt' chisa
every hour	**каждый час** kazhdyi chas
every day	**каждый день** kazhdyi dyen'
It hurts most of the time	**Болит почти все время** balit pachti fsyo vryemya
I've had it for ...	**Болит уже ...** balit uzhe
one hour/one day	**целый час/ день** tselyi chas/ dyen'
two hours/two days	**два часа/ два дня** dva chisa/ dva dnya
The pain is ...	**Боль ...** bol'
sharp	**острая** ostraya
dull	**тупая** toupaya
nagging	**ноющая** noyushaya
I feel dizzy	**У меня кружится голова** u minya kruzhitsa galava
I feel sick	**Меня тошнит** minya tashnit
I feel weak	**У меня слабость** u minya slabast'

I feel feverish	**Меня знобит** min*ya* znab*i*t
I have a temperature	**У меня температура** u min*ya* timpirat*u*ra
I am unwell	**Мне плохо** mnye pl*o*kha

Already under treatment for something else?

I take ... regularly [*show*]	**Я регулярно принимаю ...** ya rigul*ya*rna prinim*a*yu
this medicine	**это лекарство** *e*ta lik*a*rstva
these pills	**эти таблетки** *e*ti tabl*ye*tki
I have ...	**У меня ...** u min*ya*
haemorrhoids	**геморрой** ghimar*o*i
rheumatism	**ревматизм** rivmat*i*zm
I'm ...	**У меня ...** u min*ya*
diabetic	**диабет** diab*ye*t
asthmatic	**астма** *a*sma
I'm pregnant	**Я беременна** ya bir*ye*minna
I have a heart condition	**Я сердечник/ сердечница** ya sird*ye*chnik/ sird*ye*chnitsa
I am allergic to (penicillin)	**У меня аллергия на (пеницилин)** u min*ya* alirgh*i*ya na pinitsil*i*n

Other essential expressions

Please can you help?	**Помогите пожалуйста** pamaghiti pazhalusta
A doctor, please	**Врача, пожалуйста** vracha pazhalusta
A dentist	**Зубной врач** zubnoi vrach
I don't speak Russian	**Я не говорю по-русски** ya ni gavaryu pa-ruski
What time does ... arrive?	**Когда будет ...?** kagda budit
the doctor	**врач** vrach
the dentist	**зубной врач** zubnoi vrach

From the doctor: key sentences to understand

Take this ...	**Принимайте это ...** prinimaitye eta
every day/hour	**каждый день/ час** kazhdyi dyen'/ chas
twice/four times a day	**два/ четыре раза в день** dva/ chityri raza v-dyen'
Stay in bed	**Вам нужно лежать** vam nuzhna lizhat'
Don't travel	**Лучше никуда не ездить ...** luchshe nikuda ni-yezdit'
for a few days	**несколько дней** nyeskal'ka dnyei
for a week	**неделю** nidyelyu
You must go to hospital	**Вам придется лечь в больницу** vam pridyotsa lyech v-bal'nitsu

Problems: complaints, loss, theft

ESSENTIAL INFORMATION

- Problems with:
  camping facilities, see p. 33
  household appliances, see p. 46
  health, see p. 77
  the car, see p. 91
- If you are staying at the hotel, and you need some information ask someone at the reception to help you.
- If the worst comes to the worst, ask a policeman, there are plenty of them around. People in the street are usually quite helpful too.

COMPLAINTS

I bought this ...	**Я купил это ...** ya kupil eta
today	**сегодня** sivodnya
yesterday	**вчера** fchira
on Monday	**в понедельник** f-panidyel'nik

[*For days of the week, see p. 114*]

It's no good	**Эта вещь бракованная** eta vyesh brakovanaya
It's not working	**Не работает** ni rabotait
Look	**Посмотрите** pasmatriti
Here [*point*]	**Вот здесь** vot zdyes'
Can you ...	**Вы не могли бы ...** vy ni magli by
change it?	**поменять** paminyat'
mend it?	**починить** pachinit'

Here's the receipt	**Вот квитанция**
	vot kvitantsiya
Can I see the manager?	**Позовите, пожалуйста,**
	заведующего
	pazaviti pazhalusta
	zavyedushiva

LOSS

[*See also 'Theft' below; the lists are interchangeable*]

I have lost ...	**Я потерял/ потеряла ...**
	ya patiryal/patiryala
my bag	**сумку**
	sumku
my bracelet	**браслет**
	braslyet
my camera	**фотоаппарат**
	fotaaparat
my driving licence	**права**
	prava
my insurance certificate	**страховку**
	strakhofku
my jewellery	**драгоценности**
	dragatsennasti
everything	**все**
	fsyo

THEFT

[*See also 'Loss' above; the lists are interchangeable*]

Someone has stolen ...	**У меня украли ...**
	u minya ukrali
my car	**машину**
	mashinu
my car radio	**радио из машины**
	radio iz mashiny
my car keys	**ключи от машины**
	klyuchi at mashiny

my keys	**ключи** klyuch*i*
my money	**деньги** d*y*en'ghi
my necklace	**ожерелье** azhir*y*el'ye
my passport	**паспорт** paspart
my radio	**транзистор** tranz*i*ster
my tickets	**билеты** bil*y*ety
my traveller's cheques	**чеки** ch*y*eki
my wallet	**бумажник** bum*a*zhnik
my watch	**часы** chis*y*
my luggage	**багаж** bag*a*sh

LIKELY REACTIONS: key words to understand

Wait	**Подождите** padazhd*i*tye
When?	**Когда?** kagd*a*
Where?	**Где?** gdye
Name and surname?	**Имя и фамилия?** *i*mya i fam*i*liya
Address?	**Адрес?** adris
I can't help you	**Ничем не могу вам помочь** nich*y*em ni mag*u* vam pam*o*ch
It's not possible to mend it	**Это нельзя починить** *e*ta nilz*y*a pachin*i*t'

The post office

ESSENTIAL INFORMATION

- To find a post office, see p. 21
- Key words to look for:
  ПОЧТА ТЕЛЕГРАФ ТЕЛЕФОН (post office and telecommunications)
  For stamps, postcards and envelopes look for the sign:
  ПРОДАЖА МАРОК, КОНВЕРТОВ, ОТКРЫТОК
- Postcards and envelopes can also be bought at the newsagent's, stationery shops and bookshops. The signs to look for are:
  СОЮЗПЕЧАТЬ (newsagent's)
  КНИГИ (books)
  КАНЦЕЛЯРСКИЕ ТОВАРЫ (stationery)
- Letter boxes are mainly blue, although in Moscow there are also red ones for local post.
- For poste restante you should show your passport at the counter marked **ДО ВОСТРЕБОВАНИЯ** in the main post office.
- If you want to send a telegram look for the counter marked **ПРИЕМ ТЕЛЕГРАММ**

WHAT TO SAY

To England, please

В Англию, пожалуйста
v-angliyu pazhalusta

[*Hand letters, cards or parcels over the counter*]
There are two words for 'parcel' in Russian. **БАНДЕРОЛЬ** (banderol') is a parcel weighing up to 1 kilo. If you want to send a bigger parcel the word to use is **ПОСЫЛКА** (pasylka).

To Australia

В Австралию, пожалуйста
v-afstraliyu pazhalusta

To the United States

В Америку
v-amyeriku

[*For other countries, see p. 118*]

How much is ... Сколько стоит послать ...
skol'ka stoit paslat'

this parcel to Canada? эту бандероль/посылку (в Канаду)?
etu banderol'/pasylku f-kanadu

a letter (to Australia)? это письмо (в Австралию)
eta pis'mo v-afstraliyu

a postcard (to England)? эту открытку (в Англию)
etu atkrytku v-angliyu

Air mail Авиа
avia

One stamp, please Одну марку, пожалуйста
adnu marku pazhalusta

Two stamps Две марки
dvye marki

One 10 kopek stamp Одну марку за десять копеек
adnu marku za dyesit' kapyeik

I would like ... Дайте пожалуйста ...
daitye pazhalusta

an envelope конверт
kanvyert

two envelopes два конверта
dva kanvyerta

this postcard [*point*] эту открытку
etu atkrytku

three postcards три открытки
tri atkrytki

A registered letter заказное письмо
zakaznoye pis'mo

An express letter срочное письмо
srochnaye pis'mo

I'd like to send a telegram Я хочу послать телеграмму
ya khachu paslat' tiligramu

Telephoning

ESSENTIAL INFORMATION

- The sign to look for is **ТЕЛЕФОН**
- Local phone calls are cheap – 2 kopeks – and you can speak for as long as you like. It is often difficult to get change, so if you intend to make calls it is advisable to hold on to 2 or 1 kopek pieces. Remember to put the money in first, before you lift the receiver.
- If you want to phone another city or town you should do it from the post office or, if you want to call from your hotel room, book it at the reception desk. This costs approximately 15 kopeks a minute.
- Calls abroad are expensive. The same rate applies at any time of day. Direct dialling is not available at the moment.

WHAT TO SAY

I'd like to book a call ...	**Я хочу заказать разговор ...** ya khachu zakazat' razgavor
to England	**с Англией** s-angliyei
to Canada	**с Канадой** s-kanadai
to Australia	**с Австралией** s-afstraliei
to America	**с Америкой** s-amyerikai

[For other countries, see p. 118]

I'd like to make a call ...	**Я хочу позвонить ...** ya khachu pazvanit'
to Moscow	**в Москву** v-maskvu
to Leningrad	**в Ленинград** v-liningrat
Here's the number	**Вот номер** vot nomir
How much is it?	**Сколько это стоит?** skol'ka eta stoit

Hello	**Алло!**
	al*yo*
May I speak to ...?	**Можно попросить ...?**
	m*o*zhna papras*i*t'
Extension ...	**Добавочный**
	dabavachnyi
I'm sorry I don't speak Russian	**Простите, я не говорю по-русски**
	prast*i*ti ya ni gavar*yu* pa-r*u*ski
Do you speak English?	**Вы говорите по-английски?**
	vy gavar*i*ti pa-angl*i*ski
Goodbye	**До свидания**
	da-svidan'ya
I'll try again	**Я перезвоню**
	ya pirizvan*yu*

LIKELY REACTIONS

That's 3 roubles	**С вас (три) рубля**
	s-vas (tri) rubl*ya*
Cabin number (3)	**Кабина номер (три)**
	cab*i*na n*o*mir tri
[*For numbers, see p. 109*]	
Don't hang up	**Не кладите трубку**
	ni klad*i*tye tr*u*pku
You're through	**Говорите**
	gavar*i*tye
The line is engaged	**Номер занят**
	n*o*mir z*a*nit
There is no answer	**Номер не отвечает**
	n*o*mir ni-atvich*a*it
You've got the wrong number	**Вы ошиблись номером**
	vy ash*i*blis' n*o*miram
He/she is not in	**Его/ ее нет**
	yiv*o*/ yiy*o* nyet
Try again, please	**Перезвоните, пожалуйста**
	pirizvan*i*tye pazh*a*lusta

Changing cheques and money

ESSENTIAL INFORMATION

- You can change money either at the airport or at the hotel.
- Look for these signs:
  ОБМЕН ВАЛЮТЫ (change bureau)
  BUREAU DE CHANGE
- For finding the way to the bank or exchange bureau, see p. 21.
- In the special hard currency shops for foreigners you can pay by major credit cards, but it is wise to check with the cashier first. Otherwise pay by cash. Remember that ordinary Soviet shops do not accept hard currency, only roubles.

WHAT TO SAY

I'd like to cash this traveller's cheque	**Я хочу получить по чеку** ya khachu paluchit' pa chyeku
Where can I change some money?	**Где я могу обменять валюту?** gdye ya magu abminyat' valyutu
I'd like to change this into roubles	**Я хочу обменять это на рубли** ya khachu abminyat' eta na rubli
Here's ...	**Вот ...** vot
my banker's card	**моя карточка** maya kartachka
my passport	**мой паспорт** moy paspart
What's the rate of exchange?	**Какой сейчас курс?** kakoi sichas kurs

LIKELY REACTIONS

Passport, please	**Паспорт, пожалуйста** paspart pazhalusta
Sign here	**Распишитесь здесь** raspishitis' zdyes'
Your banker's card, please	**Вашу карточку, пожалуйста** vashu kartachku pazhalusta
Go to the cash desk	**Пройдите в кассу** praiditye f-kassu

Car travel

ESSENTIAL INFORMATION

- If you travel to the USSR by car you have to confirm your itinerary in detail with the INTOURIST and stick to it. There are many traffic police road posts and your progress is normally monitored. It is advisable not to deviate from your route, even if it is only to have a picnic.
- Filling stations are few and far between, so it is best to carry one or two 5 gallon cans with you and fill them up whenever you can, just in case. High grade and diesel petrol are often in short supply.
  You normally pay for petrol with coupons (**ТАЛОНЫ**) available from Intourist).
- For finding a filling station or garage, see p. 21.

Spare parts are very hard to come by, but mechanics at the Intourist garages are quite efficient and sometimes produce spare parts on the spot.

WHAT TO SAY

For numbers, see p. 109]

Where is the nearest ...	**Где здесь ...** gdye zdyes'
petrol station?	**заправочная** zapravachnaya
garage?	**станция обслуживания** stantsiya apsluzhivaniya
Nine) litres of ...	**(Девять) литров ...** dyevit' litraf
Fill it up, please	**Полный бак, пожалуйста** polnyi bak pazhalusta

Will you check ...	**Проверьте, пожалуйста ...**
	prav*y*er'tye pazh*a*lusta
the oil	**масло**
	m*a*sla
the battery	**аккумулятор**
	akumul*y*atar
the radiator	**радиатор**
	radi*a*tr
the tyres	**шины**
	sh*i*ny
I've run out of petrol	**У меня кончился бензин**
	u min*y*a k*o*nchilsa binz*i*n
My car has broken down	**У меня сломалась машина**
	u min*y*a slamalas' mash*i*na
My car won't start	**Машина не заводится**
	mash*i*na ni zav*o*ditsa
I've had an accident	**У меня авария**
	u min*y*a av*a*riya
I've lost my car keys	**Я потерял ключи от машины**
	ya patir*y*al klyuch*i* at mash*i*ny
My car is ...	**Моя машина ...**
	ma*y*a mash*i*na
two kilometres away	**в двух километрах отсюда**
	v-dvukh kilam*y*etrakh ats*y*uda
three kilometres away	**в трех километрах отсюда**
	f-troykh kilam*y*etrakh ats*y*uda
Can you help me, please?	**Помогите, пожалуйста**
	pamagh*i*ti pazh*a*lusta
Do you do repairs?	**Здесь производится ремонт машин?**
	zdyes' praizv*o*ditsa rim*o*nt mash*i*n
I have a puncture	**У меня прокол**
	u min*y*a prak*o*l
I have a broken windscreen	**У меня разбито ветровое стекло**
	u min*y*a razb*i*ta vitrav*o*ye stikl*o*
I think the problem is here ... [*point*]	**Мне кажется, неполадка здесь**
	mnye k*a*zhitsa nipal*a*tka zdyes'

I don't know what's wrong	**Я не знаю в чем дело** ya ni znayu f-chom dyela
Can you ...	**Вы можете ...** vy mozhitye
repair the fault?	**отремонтировать** atrimantiravat'
come and look?	**посмотреть** pasmatryet'
estimate the cost?	**сказать сколько это будет стоить** skazat' skol'ka eta budit stoit'
write it down?	**это написать** eta napisat'
Do you accept these coupons?	**Вы берете такие талоны?** vy biryotye takii talony
How long will the repair take?	**Сколько времени займет ремонт?** skol'ka vryemini zaimyot rimont
When will the car be ready?	**Когда будет готова машина?** kagda budit gatova mashina
Can I see the bill?	**Можно посмотреть счет?** mozhna pasmatryet' shyot
This is my insurance document	**Вот моя страховка** vot maya strakhofka

HIRING A CAR

Can I hire a car?	**Можно взять напрокат машину?** mozhna vzyat' naprakat mashinu
I need a car ...	**Мне нужна машина ...** mnye nuzhna mashina
for two people	**на двоих** na dvaikh
for five people	**на пятерых** na pitirykh
for one day	**на сутки** na sutki

1	windscreen wipers	стеклоочистители styeklaaschistiteli
2	fuses	пробки propki
3	heater	обогреватель abagrivatyel'
4	battery	аккумулятор akumulyatar
5	engine	мотор matór
6	fuel pump	бензиновый насос binzinavyi nasos
7	starter motor	стартер statyer
8	carburettor	карбюратор karbyurater
9	lights	фары fary
10	radiator	радиатор radiatr

11	fan belt	приводной ремень privadno rimyen'
12	generator	генератор giniratr
13	brakes	тормоза tarmaza
14	clutch	сцепление stsiplyen'ye
15	gear box	коробка скоростей karopka skarastye
16	steering	руль rul'
17	ignition	зажигание zazhigan'ye
18	transmission	передача piridacha
19	exhaust	выхлопная труба vykhlapnaya truba
20	indicators	указатели ukazatili

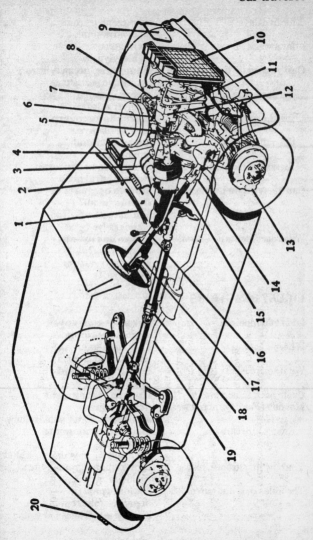

for five days	**на пятеро суток** na pyatira sutak
for a week	**на неделю** na nidyelyu
Can you write down?	**Напишите, пожалуйста** napishitye pazhalusta
the deposit to pay	**размер залога** razmyer zaloga
the charge per kilometre?	**тариф за километр** tarif za kilamyetr
the daily charge?	**дневной тариф** dnivnoi tarif
the cost of insurance?	**стоимость страховки** stoimast' strakhofki
Can I leave it (in Leningrad)	**Можно оставить ее (в Ленинграде)?** mozhna astavit' yiyo vliningradye
What documents do I need?	**Какие мне нужны документы?** kakii mnye nuzhny dakumyenty

LIKELY REACTIONS

I don't do repairs	**Мы не ремонтируем** my ni rimantiruim
Where's your car?	**Где ваша машина?** gdye vasha mashina
What make is it?	**Какой она марки?** kakoi ana marki
Come back tomorrow/on Monday [*For days of the week, see p. 114*]	**Приходите завтра/ в понедельник** prikhaditi zaftra/f-panidyel'nik
We don't hire cars	**Мы не даем машины напрокат** my ni dayom mashiny naprakat
Your driving licence, please	**Ваши права, пожалуйста** vashi prava pazhalusta
The mileage is unlimited	**Километраж не ограничивается** kilamitrash ni agranichvaitsa

Public transport

ESSENTIAL INFORMATION

- Public transport in the USSR is cheap. You pay a flat charge of 5 kopeks (about 5 pence) for any length of journey on a bus, underground, trolleybus or tram. For bus, trolleybus and tram you should get a book of special tickets from a newsagent's (sometimes the driver sells them, but it is best not to rely on that). In some places there are minibuses which follow a certain route and stop at the request of individual passengers. They are called **МАРШРУТНЫЕ ТАКСИ** and cost 15 kopeks.
- Underground is fast, clean and efficient, and by far the best way of travel in the big cities.
- Taxis are not as expensive as they are in the West, but it is often difficult to find one, and then to persuade them to take you where you want to go. The best thing to do is to get in and then tell the driver the destination. There are also quite a lot of private car owners who work as taxi drivers in their spare time to earn extra cash.
- State-run taxis are usually marked with a letter T and have a chequered design on the side.
- Most of the railway stations have two sections. One is for long distance journeys and is called **ПОЕЗДА ДАЛЬНЕГО СЛЕДОВАНИЯ**.
- The section called **ПРИГОРОДНЫЕ ПОЕЗДА** is for shorter journeys.
- Local trains are called **ЭЛЕКТРИЧКА** (iliktrichka).
- Long distance trains vary according to speed. The slowest is **ПАССАЖИРСКИЙ ПОЕЗД**. It is probably better to take a **СКОРЫЙ** (fast train) or an **ЭКСПРЕСС**. Both stop only at main stations and are reasonably comfortable.
- The carriages are also graded:

МЯГКИЙ ВАГОН
myakhkii vagon
— a sleeper with compartments for two people, usually providing individual washing facilities.

КУПЕЙНЫЙ ВАГОН
kupeynyi vagon
— a sleeper with compartments for four people.

- Restaurant car **ВАГОН РЕСТОРАН** is usually available on fast trains. However, Russians normally take their own food for the journey. The carriage attendant **ПРОВОДНИК,** or **ПРОВОДНИЦА** if it is a woman, brings tea several times a day on long distance journeys.
- Key words on signs:
  КАССА (ticket office)
  КАМЕРА ХРАНЕНИЯ (left luggage)
  ВХОД (entrance)
  ВЫХОД (exit)
  РАСПИСАНИЕ ПОЕЗДОВ (timetable)
  ПЛАТФОРМА (platform)
  СПРАВОЧНОЕ БЮРО (information office)
  ПРИБЫТИЕ ПОЕЗДОВ (arrival of trains)
  ОТПРАВЛЕНИЕ ПОЕЗДОВ (departure)

WHAT TO SAY

Where does the train for (Moscow) leave from?	**С какого пути отправляется поезд на (Москву)?** s-kakova puti atpravlyaitsa poist na (maskvu)
At what time does the train leave for (Moscow)?	**В котором часу отходит поезд на (Москву)?** f-katoram chisu atkhodit poist na (maskvu)
At what time does the train from (Leningrad) arrive?	**В котором часу приходит поезд из (Ленинграда)?** f-katoram chisu prikhodit poist iz (liningrada)
Does the train for (Kiev) leave from this platform?	**Скажите, поезд на (Киев) отходит с этого пути?** skazhitye poist na (kiif) atkhodit s etava puti
Does this train go to ... ?	**Скажите, эта электричка идет в ...?** skazhitye eta iliktrichka idyot v
Does this train stop at ... ?	**Эта электричка останавливается в ...?** eta iliktrichka astanavlivaitsa v

Which station do trains for ... go from?	**С какого вокзала идут поезда на ...?** s-kakova vakzala idut paizda na
I need a ticket for ...	**Дайте, пожалуйста, один билет до ...** daytye pazhalusta adin bilyet da
Two tickets	**Два билета** dva bilyeta
Return ticket	**Туда и обратно** tuda i abratna
Adult ticket	**Взрослый билет** vzroslyi bilyet
Half fare (for a child)	**Детский билет** dyetskii bilyet
How do I get to ... please?	**Скажите, как мне добраться до ...?** skazhitye kak mnye dabratsa da
the hotel	**гостиницы** gastinitsy
the airport	**аэровокзала** airavakzala
the station	**вокзала** vakzala
the museum	**музея** muzeya
the theatre	**театра** tiatra
the beach	**пляжа** plyazha
the town centre	**центра** tsentra
the market place	**рынка** rynka

Is this ...	Этот ...
	etat
the bus for the market place?	**автобус идет до рынка?**
	aftobus idyot da rynka
the tram for the railway station?	**трамвай идет до вокзала?**
	tramvai idyot da vakzala
Where can I get a taxi?	**Где стоянка такси?**
	gdye stayanka taksi
Can you put me off at the right stop, please?	**Вы не скажете, когда мне выходить?**
	vy ni skazhitye kagda mnye vykhadit'
Can I book a seat?	**Можно заказать билет?**
	mozhna zakazat' bilyet
A single	**Туда**
	tuda
A return	**Туда и обратно**
	tuda i abratna
One adult	**Один взрослый**
	adin vzroslyi
Two adults	**Два взрослых**
	dva vzroslykh
and one child	**и один детский**
	i adin dyetskii
and two children	**и два детских**
	i dva dyetskikh
How much is it?	**Сколько это стоит?**
	skol'ka eta stoit

Buses, trolleybuses and underground tend to get crowded, so when your stop approaches you have to make your way towards the exit. The best way to do it is to say:

Вы выходите на следующей?	Are you getting out at the next stop?
vy vykhoditye na slyedushei	

or:

Разрешите пройти	Excuse me
razrishitye praiti	

LIKELY REACTIONS

Over there	**Вон там** von tam
Here	**Здесь** zdyes'
Platform (One)	**Первый путь** pyervyi put'
At (four o'clock)	**В четыре часа** f-chityri chisa
[For times, see p. 111]	
Change at ... station	**Сделайте пересадку на станции ...** zdyelaitye pirisatku na stantsii
Go as far as ...	**Доезжайте до ...** daizzhaitye da
And then ask	**И там спросите** i tam sprasitye
This is your stop	**Вам сейчас выходить** vam sichas vykhadit'

Leisure

ESSENTIAL INFORMATION

- For finding the way to a place of entertainment, see p. 21.
- For times of day, see p. 111.
- For important signs, see p. 107.
- Cinema and theatre tickets are usually cheap, but often difficult to get if you want to see something special. If you absolutely have to see a ballet at the Kirov or Bolshoi it is best to book through the ticket desk at your hotel. You are more likely to get tickets if you are prepared to pay in **ВАЛЮТА** (hard currency).
- Nightlife is virtually non-existent in the USSR and there are very few discos around.

WHAT TO SAY

At what time does ... open?	**В котором часу открывается ...?**
	f-katoram chisu atkryvaitsa
the art gallery	**картинная галерея**
	kartinnaya galiryeya
the museum	**музей**
	muzei
the swimming pool	**бассейн**
	basein
the zoo	**зоопарк**
	zaapark
the skating rink	**каток**
	katok
When is the next showing?	**Когда начинается следующий сеанс?**
	kagda nachinaitsa slyedushii sians
At what time does ... close?	**Когда закрывается ...?**
	kagda zakryvaitsa
At what time does ... start?	**Когда начинается ...?**
	kagda nachinaitsa

[See also above list]

the concert	**концерт** kantsert
the match	**матч** match
the performance	**спектакль** spiktakl'
How much is it ...	**Сколько стоит билет ...?** skol'ka stoit bilyet
for an adult?	**для взрослых** dlya vzroslykh
for a child?	**для детей** dlya dityei
Two adults, please	**Два билета для взрослых, пожалуйста** dva bilyeta dlya vzroslykh pazhalusta
Three children, please	**Три детских, пожалуйста** tri dyetskikh pazhalusta
In the stalls	**В партере** f-parterye

If you cannot manage to get tickets for the performance you want to see you could always try what most Russians do when the tickets are sold out – stand outside the theatre before the beginning of the performance and ask for a spare ticket. Here is what you say:

У вас нет лишнего билета? u vas nyet lishniva bilyeta	Have you got a spare ticket?
Do you have ...	**У вас есть ...?** u vas yest'
a programme?	**программа** pragrama
tickets for tomorrow?	**билеты на завтра** bilyety na zaftra
tickets for today?	**билеты на сегодня** bilyety na sivodnya
a guide book?	**путеводитель** putivaditil'

Where's the toilet, please?	**Скажите пожалуйста, где туалет?** skazhitye pazhalusta gdye tualyet
Where's the cloakroom?	**Где гардероб?** gdye gardirop
Can I hire ...	**Можно взять напрокат ...** mozhna vzyat' naprakat
some skis?	**лыжи?** lyzhi
a boat?	**лодку?** lotku
skates?	**коньки?** kan'ki
a deck-chair?	**шезлонг?** shizlonk
rackets?	**ракетки?** rakyetki
a sun umbrella?	**тент?** tent
How much is it ...	**Сколько это стоит ...** skol'ka eta stoit
per day/per hour?	**в день/ в час?** v-dyen'/ f-chas

Asking if things are allowed

WHAT TO SAY

Excuse me, please	**Простите, пожалуйста** prastitye pazhalusta
May one ... here?	**Здесь можно ...?** zdyes' mozhna
camp	**устроить стоянку** ustroit' stayanku
pitch a tent	**поставить палатку** pastavit' palatku
fish	**ловить рыбу** lavit' rybu
park	**поставить машину** pastavit' mashinu
smoke	**курить** kurit'
swim	**купаться** kupatsa
Can I ...	**Можно ...** mozhna
come in?	**войти** vaiti
leave my things here?	**здесь оставить вещи** zdyes' astavit' vyeshi
look around?	**посмотреть** pasmatryet'
sit here?	**сесть** syest'
take photos here?	**снимать** snimat'
telephone here?	**позвонить** pazvanit'
wait here?	**здесь подождать** zdyes' padazhdat'

LIKELY REACTIONS

Yes, certainly	**Да, конечно** da kanyeshna
Help yourself	**Пожалуйста** pazhalusta
I think so	**Думаю, что да** dumayu shto da
Yes, you can	**Да, можно** da mozhna
Yes, but be careful	**Да, но будьте осторожны** da no but'tye astarozhny
No, certainly not	**Нет, нельзя** nyet, nil'zya
I don't think so	**Думаю что нет** dumayu shto nyet
I don't know	**Не знаю** ni znayu
Sorry	**Простите** prastitye

Reference

PUBLIC NOTICES

- Key words on signs for drivers, pedestrians, travellers and shoppers.

ВСЕ БИЛЕТЫ ПРОДАНЫ fsye bilyety prodany	Tickets sold out
ВХОД (ВЪЕЗД) **ЗАПРЕЩЕН** fkhot (v'yest) zaprishyon	No entry
ЗАКРЫТО zakryta	Closed
ЗАЛ ОЖИДАНИЯ zal azhidan'ya	Waiting room
ЗАПАСНОЙ ВЫХОД zapasnoi vykhat	Emergency exit
ЗАПРЕЩАЕТСЯ zaprishaitsa	Forbidden
К СЕБЕ k-sibye	Pull
ОСТОРОЖНО astarozhna	Look out
НЕ КУРИТЬ ni kurit'	No smoking
ОКРАШЕНО akrashina	Wet paint
ОПАСНО ДЛЯ ЖИЗНИ apasna dlya zhizni	Danger of death
ОТ СЕБЯ at sibya	Push
ПЕРЕХОД pirikhot	Subway
ПЕРЕРЫВ piriryf	Lunch break
ПО ГАЗОНАМ НЕ **ХОДИТЬ** pa gazonam ni khadit'	Do not walk on grass

ПОСТОРОННИМ ВХОД ВОСПРЕЩЕН	Private
pastaronnim fkhot vasprishon	
НЕ ПРИСЛОНЯТЬСЯ	Do not lean
ni prislanyatsa	
РУКАМИ НЕ ТРОГАТЬ	Do not touch
rukami ni trogat'	
САМООБСЛУЖИВАНИЕ	Self-service
sama-apsluzhivaniye	
СТРОГО ВОСПРЕЩАЕТСЯ	Strictly forbidden
stroga vasprishaitsa	
ТУАЛЕТ (Ж)	Ladies
tualyet	
ТУАЛЕТ (М)	Gentlemen
tualyet	

ABBREVIATIONS

г.	год	year
г.	город	city/town
г.	грамм	grammes
д.	дом	house
ж.	женский	ladies
и. т. д.	и так далее	etc.
кв.	квартира	flat
км.	километр	kilometre
коп.	копейка	kopeck
л.	литр	litre
м.	метр	metre
м./мин.	минут	minutes
пер.	переулок	lane
пл.	площадь	square
просп.	проспект	avenue
руб.	рубль	rouble
Св.	святой	Saint
см.	сантиметр	centimetre
ст.	станция	station
тов.	товарищ	comrade
ул.	улица	street
ч.	часов	hour

NUMBERS

Cardinal numbers

0	ноль	nol'
1	один	adin
2	два	dva
3	три	tri
4	четыре	chityri
5	пять	pyat'
6	шесть	shest'
7	семь	syem'
8	восемь	vosim'
9	девять	dyevit'
10	десять	dyesit'
11	одиннадцать	adinatsit'
12	двенадцать	dvinatsit'
13	тринадцать	trinatsit'
14	четырнадцать	chityrnatsit'
15	пятнадцать	pitnatsit'
16	шестнадцать	shisnatsit'
17	семнадцать	simnatsit'
18	восемнадцать	vasimnatsit'
19	девятнадцать	divitnatsit'
20	двадцать	dvatsit'
21	двадцать один	dvatsit' adin
22	двадцать два	dvatsit' dva
23	двадцать три	dvatsit' tri
24	двадцать четыре	dvatsit' chityri
25	двадцать пять	dvatsit' pyat'
26	двадцать шесть	dvatsit' shest'
27	двадцать семь	dvatsit' syem'
28	двадцать восемь	dvatsit' vosim'
29	двадцать девять	dvatsit' dyevit'
30	тридцать	tritsit'
35	тридцать пять	tritsit' pyat'
38	тридцать восемь	tritsit' vosim'
40	сорок	sorak
41	сорок один	sorak adin
45	сорок пять	sorak pyat'
48	сорок восемь	sorak vosim'

50	**пятьдесят**	piddisyat
55	**пятьдесят пять**	piddisyat pyat'
56	**пятьдесят шесть**	piddisyat shest'
60	**шестьдесят**	shizdisyat
65	**шестьдесят пять**	shizdisyat pyat'
70	**семьдесят**	syem'disit
75	**семьдесят пять**	syem'disit pyat'
80	**восемьдесят**	vosimdisit
85	**восемьдесят пять**	vosimdisit pyat'
90	**девяносто**	divinosta
95	**девяносто пять**	divinosta pyat'
100	**сто**	sto
101	**сто один**	sto adin
102	**сто два**	sto dva
125	**сто двадцать пять**	sto dvatsit' pyat'
150	**сто пятьдесят**	sto piddisyat
175	**сто семьдесят пять**	sto syem'disit pyat'
200	**двести**	dvyesti
300	**триста**	trista
400	**четыреста**	chityrista
500	**пятьсот**	pitsot
600	**шестьсот**	shissot
1,000	**тысяча**	tysicha
1,500	**тысяча пятьсот**	tysicha pitsot
2,000	**две тысячи**	dvye tysichi
5,000	**пять тысяч**	pyat' tysich
10,000	**десять тысяч**	dyesit' tysich
100,000	**сто тысяч**	sto tysich
1,000,000	**миллион**	mil'yon

Ordinal numbers

1st	**первый**	pyervyi
2nd	**второй**	ftaroi
3rd	**третий**	tryetii
4th	**четвертый**	chitvyortyi
5th	**пятый**	pyatyi
6th	**шестой**	shistoi
7th	**седьмой**	sid'moi
8th	**восьмой**	vas'moi
9th	**девятый**	divyatyi
10th	**десятый**	disyatyi
11th	**одиннадцатый**	adinatsatyi
12th	**двенадцатый**	dvinatsatyi

TIME

What time is it?	**Который час?**
	katoryi chas
It's ...	**Сейчас**
	sichas
one o'clock	**час**
	chas
two o'clock	**два часа**
	dva chisa
three o'clock	**три часа**
	tri chisa
four o'clock	**четыре часа**
	chityri chisa
five o'clock	**пять часов**
	pyat' chisof
six o'clock	**шесть часов**
	shest' chisof
in the morning	**утра**
	utra
in the afternoon	**дня**
	dnya
in the evening	**вечера**
	vyechira
at night	**ночи**
	nochi

It's ...	Сейчас
	sichas
noon	полдень
	poldin'
midnight	полночь
	polnych
It's ...	Сейчас
	sichas
five past one	пять минут второго
	pyat' minut ftarova
ten past two	десять минут третьего
	dyesit' minut tryetiva
a quarter past three	четверть четвертого
	chyetvirt' chitvyortava
twenty past four	двадцать минут пятого
	dvatsit' minut pyatava
twenty-five past five	двадцать пять минут
	шестого
	dvatsit' pyat' minut shistova
half past six	половина седьмого
	palavina sid'mova
seven	восьмого
	vas'mova
eight	девятого
	divyatava
nine	десятого
	disyatava
ten	одиннадцатого
	adinatsatava
eleven	двенадцатого
	dvinatsatava
twelve	первого
	pyervava
twenty-five to seven	без двадцати пяти семь
	biz dvatsiti piti syem'
twenty to eight	без двадцати восемь
	biz dvatsiti vosim'
a quarter to nine	без четверти девять
	bis-chyetvirti dyevit'
ten to ten	без десяти десять
	biz disiti dyesit'

five to eleven	**без пяти одиннадцать** bis-pit*i* ad*i*natsat'
At what time .... (does the train leave)?	**В котором часу ... (отходит поезд)?** f kat*o*ram chis*u* atkh*o*dit p*o*ist
At ...	**B ...** v
13.00	**тринадцать часов** trinatsat' chis*of*
14.05	**четырнадцать часов пять минут** cht*y*rnatsat' chis*of* pyat' min*u*t
15.10	**пятнадцать часов десять минут** pitnatsat' chis*of* d*y*esit' min*u*t
16.15	**шестнадцать часов пятнадцать минут** shisnatsat' chis*of* pitnatsat' min*u*t
17.20	**семнадцать часов двадцать минут** simnatsat' chis*of* dv*a*tsat' min*u*t
18.25	**восемнадцать часов двадцать пять минут** vasimnatsat' chis*of* dvatsat pyat' min*u*t
19.30	**девятнадцать часов тридцать минут** divitnatsat' chis*of* tr*i*tsat' min*u*t
20.35	**двадцать часов тридцать пять минут** dvatsat' chis*of* tr*i*sat' pyat' min*u*t
21.40	**двадцать один час сорок минут** dvatsat' ad*i*n chas s*o*rak min*u*t
22.45	**двадцать два часа сорок пять минут** dvatsat' dva chis*a* s*o*rak pyat' min*u*t

23.50	**двадцать три часа пятьдесят минут** dvatsat' tri chisa piddisyat minut
00.55	**двадцать четыре часа пятьдесят пять минут** dvatsat' chityri chisa piddisyat pyat' minut
In ten minutes	**Через десять минут** chyeris dyesit' minut
In a quarter of an hour	**Через четверть часа** chyeris chyetvirt' chisa
In half an hour	**Через полчаса** chyeris pol-chisa
In three-quarters of an hour	**Через сорок пять минут** chyeris sorak pyat' minut
In an hour	**Через час** chyeris chas

DAYS

Monday	**Понедельник** panidyel'nik
Tuesday	**Вторник** ftornik
Wednesday	**Среда** srida
Thursday	**Четверг** chitvyerk
Friday	**Пятница** pyatnitsa
Saturday	**Суббота** subota
Sunday	**Воскресенье** vaskrisyen'ye
last Monday	**в прошлый понедельник** f-proshlyi panidyel'nik
next Tuesday	**в следующий вторник** f-slyeduyushii ftornik
on Wednesday	**в среду** f-sryedu

on Thursdays	**по четвергам** pa chitvirgam
until Friday	**до пятницы** da pyatnitsy
before Saturday	**до субботы** da suboty
after Sunday	**после воскресенья** poslye vaskrisyen'ya
the day before yesterday	**позавчера** pazafchira
two days ago	**два дня назад** dva dnya nazat
yesterday	**вчера** fchira
yesterday morning	**вчера утром** fchira utram
yesterday afternoon	**вчера днем** fchira dnyom
last night	**вчера вечером** fchira vyechiram
today	**сегодня** sivodnya
this morning	**сегодня утром** sivodnya utram
this afternoon	**(сегодня) днем** sivodnya dnyom
tonight	**сегодня вечером** sivodnya vyechiram
tomorrow	**завтра** zaftra
tomorrow morning	**завтра утром** saftra utram
tomorrow afternoon	**завтра днем** zaftra dnyom
tomorrow evening	**завтра вечером** zaftra vyechiram
tomorrow night	**завтра ночью** zaftra noch'yu
the day after tomorrow	**послезавтра** poslizaftra

MONTHS AND DATES
(including public holidays)

January	**Январь** yinvar'
February	**Февраль** fivral'
March	**Март** mart
April	**Апрель** apryel'
May	**Май** mai
June	**Июнь** eeyun'
July	**Июль** eeyul'
August	**Август** avgust
September	**Сентябрь** sintyabr'
October	**Октябрь** aktyabr'
November	**Ноябрь** nayabr'
December	**Декабрь** dikabr'
in January	**в январе** v-yinvarye
until February	**до февраля** da fivralya
before March	**до марта** da marta
after April	**после апреля** poslye apryela
during May	**в мае** v-mahye
not until June	**не раньше июня** ni-ran'she eeyunya
in the beginning of July	**в начале июля** v-nachalye eeyulya

in the middle of August	**в середине августа**
	f-siridinye avgusta
at the end of September	**в конце сентября**
	f-kantse sintibrya
last month	**в прошлом месяце**
	f proshlam myesitse
this month	**в этом месяце**
	v-etam myesitse
next month	**в следующем месяце**
	f-slyeduyushyem myesitse
in spring	**весной**
	visnoi
in summer	**летом**
	lyetam
in autumn	**осенью**
	osin'yu
in winter	**зимой**
	zimoi
this year	**в этом году**
	v-etam gadu
last year	**в прошлом году**
	f-proshlam gadu
next year	**в следующем году**
	f-slyeduyushyem gadu
in 1983	**в восемьдесят третьем году**
	v-vosimdisit tryet'yem gadu
in 1989	**в восемьдесят девятом году**
	v-vosimdisyat divyatam gadu
in 1992	**в девяносто втором году**
	v-divinosta ftarom gadu
What's the date today?	**Какое сегодня число?**
	kakoye sivodnya chislo
It's the 6th of March	**Шестое марта**
	shistoye marta
It's the 12th April	**двенадцатое апреля**
	dvinatsataye apryelya
It's the 21st of August	**двадцать первое августа**
	dvatsat' pyervaye avgusta

Public holidays

On these days offices, shops and schools are closed:

1st January	Новый год	New Year's Day
8th March	Женский день	Women's Day
1st & 2nd May	Первое мая	Labour days
9th May	День победы	Victory day
7th October	День конституции	Constitution day
7th & 8th November	Седьмое ноября	Revolution days

COUNTRIES AND NATIONALITIES

Countries

Australia	**Австралия** afstraliya
Austria	**Австрия** afstriya
Belgium	**Бельгия** byel'ghiya
Britain	**Великобритания** vilikabritaniya
Canada	**Канада** canada
East Africa	**Восточная Африка** vastochnaya africa
Eire	**Ирландия** irlandiya
England	**Англия** angliya
France	**Франция** frantsiya
Greece	**Греция** gryetsiya
India	**Индия** indiya

Italy	**Италия**
	italiya
Luxembourg	**Люксембург**
	lyuksimburk
Netherlands	**Голландия**
	gallandiya
New Zealand	**Новая Зеландия**
	novaya zilandiya
Northern Ireland	**Северная Ирландия**
	syevirnaya irlandiya
Pakistan	**Пакистан**
	pakistan
Portugal	**Португалия**
	partugaliya
Scotland	**Шотландия**
	shatlandiya
South Africa	**ЮАР**
	yuar
Spain	**Испания**
	ispaniya
Switzerland	**Швейцария**
	shvitsariya
United States	**США / Америка**
	Se-Shae-Ah/Amyerica
Wales	**Уэльс**
	ouel's
West Germany	**Западная Германия**
	zapadnaya ghirmaniya
West Indies	**Вест-Индия**
	vest indiya

Nationalities

American	**американец/ американка**
	amirikanyets/ amiricanka
Australian	**австралиец/ австралийка**
	afstraliyets/ afstralīka
British	**британец/ британка**
	britanyets/ britanka
Canadian	**канадец/ канадка**
	canadits/ canatca
East African	**из Восточной Африки**
	iz vastochnai afriki
English	**англичанин/ англичанка**
	anglichanin/ anglichanka
Indian	**индиец/ индианка**
	indiyets/ indianka
Irish	**ирландец/ ирландка**
	irlandyets/ irlanka
a New Zealander	**новозеландец/**
	новозеландка
	navazilandyets/ navazilanka
a Pakistani	**пакистанец/ пакистанка**
	pakistanyets/ pakistanka
Scots	**шотландец/ шотландка**
	shatlandyets/ shatlanka
South African	**из ЮАР**
	iz yuar
Welsh	**валлиец/ валлийка**
	valiyets/ valīka
West Indian	**из Вест-Индии**
	iz vest-īndii

DEPARTMENT STORE GUIDE

Второй	First floor
Детская одежда	Children's wear
Галантерея	Haberdashery
Готовая одежда	Ready-made clothing
Головные уборы	Millinery
Женская одежда	Ladies' wear

Игрушки	Toys
Касса	Checkout
Канцелярские товары	Stationery
Керамика	Earthenware
Книги	Books
Ковры	Carpets
Кожгалантерея	Leather goods
Косметика	Cosmetics
Мебель	Furniture
Мужская одежда	Menswear
Меха	Fur
Обувь	Footwear
Отдел	Department
Парфюмерия	Perfumery
Первый	Ground floor
Пластинки	Records
Подарки	Gifts
Посуда	Crockery
Продукты	Food
Радиотовары	Radio
Спорттовары	Sports
Строчевышитые изделия	Table and bed-linen
Стекло	Glassware
Сувениры	Souvenirs
Телевизоры	Television
Ткани	Fabrics
Третий	Second floor
Трикотаж	Pullovers
Фарфор	China
Фототовары	Photography
Хозяйственные товары	Kitchen utensils & hardware
Часы	Watches
Четвертый	Third floor
Чулки-носки	Hosiery
Ювелирные товары	Jewellery
Электротовары	Electric appliances
Этаж	Floor

CONVERSION TABLES

Read the centre column of these tables from right to left to convert from metric to imperial and from left to right to convert from imperial to metric e.g. 5 litres = 8.80 pints; 5 pints = 2.84 litres.

pints		litres	gallons		litres
1.76	1	0.57	0.22	1	4.55
3.52	2	1.14	0.44	2	9.09
5.28	3	1.70	0.66	3	13.64
7.07	4	2.27	0.88	4	18.18
8.80	5	2.84	1.00	5	22.73
10.56	6	3.41	1.32	6	27.28
12.32	7	3.98	1.54	7	31.82
14.08	8	4.55	1.76	8	36.37
15.84	9	5.11	1.98	9	40.91

ounces		grams	pounds		kilos
0.04	1	28.35	2.20	1	0.45
0.07	2	56.70	4.41	2	0.91
0.11	3	85.05	6.61	3	1.36
0.14	4	113.40	8.82	4	1.81
0.18	5	141.75	11.02	5	2.27
0.21	6	170.10	13.23	6	2.72
0.25	7	198.45	15.43	7	3.18
0.28	8	226.80	17.64	8	3.63
0.32	9	255.15	19.84	9	4.08

inches		centimetres	yards		metres
0.39	1	2.54	1.09	1	0.91
0.79	2	5.08	2.19	2	1.83
1.18	3	7.62	3.28	3	2.74
1.58	4	10.16	4.37	4	3.66
1.95	5	12.70	5.47	5	4.57
2.36	6	15.24	6.56	6	5.49
2.76	7	17.78	7.66	7	6.40
3.15	8	20.32	8.65	8	7.32
3.54	9	22.86	9.84	9	8.23

miles		kilometres
0.62	1	1.61
1.24	2	3.22
1.86	3	4.83
2.49	4	6.44
3.11	5	8.05
3.73	6	9.66
4.35	7	11.27
4.97	8	12.87
5.59	9	14.48

A quick way to convert kilometres to miles: divide by 8 and multiply by 5. To convert miles to kilometres: divide by 5 and multiply by 8.

fahrenheit (°F)	centigrade (°C)	lbs/ sq in	k/ sq cm
212°	100° boiling point	18	1.3
100°	38°	20	1.4
98.4°	36.9° body temperature	22	1.5
86°	30°	25	1.7
77°	25°	29	2.0
68°	20°	32	2.3
59°	15°	35	2.5
50°	10°	36	2.5
41°	5°	39	2.7
32°	0° freezing point	40	2.8
14°	−10°	43	3.0
−4°	−20°	45	3.2
		46	3.2
		50	3.5
		60	4.2

To convert °C to °F: divide by 5, multiply by 9 and add 32.
To convert °F to °C: take away 32, divide by 9 and multiply by 5.

CLOTHING SIZES

Remember – always try on clothes before buying. Clothing sizes are usually unreliable.

women's dresses and suits

Europe	38	40	42	44	46	48
UK	32	34	36	38	40	42
USA	10	12	14	16	18	20

men's suits and coats

Europe	46	48	50	52	54	56
UK and USA	36	38	40	42	44	46

men's shirts

Europe	36	37	38	39	41	42	43
UK and USA	14	14½	15	15½	16	16½	17

socks

Europe	38-39	39-40	40-41	41-42	42-43
UK and USA	9½	10	10½	11	11½

shoes

Europe	34	35½	36½	38	39	41	42	43	44	45
UK	2	3	4	5	6	7	8	9	10	11
USA	3½	4½	5½	6½	7½	8½	9½	10½	11½	12½

Index

All Pan books are available at your local bookshop or newsagent, or can be ordered direct from the publisher. Indicate the number of copies required and fill in the form below.

Send to: **CS Department, Pan Books Ltd., P.O. Box 40,
              Basingstoke, Hants. RG21 2YT.**

or phone: 0256 469551 (Ansaphone), quoting title, author
              and Credit Card number.

Please enclose a remittance* to the value of the cover price plus: 60p for the first book plus 30p per copy for each additional book ordered to a maximum charge of £2.40 to cover postage and packing.

*Payment may be made in sterling by UK personal cheque, postal order, sterling draft or international money order, made payable to Pan Books Ltd.

Alternatively by Barclaycard/Access:

Card No.

Signature:

Applicable only in the UK and Republic of Ireland.

While every effort is made to keep prices low, it is sometimes necessary to increase prices at short notice. Pan Books reserve the right to show on covers and charge new retail prices which may differ from those advertised in the text or elsewhere.

NAME AND ADDRESS IN BLOCK LETTERS PLEASE:

....

Name ————————————————————————————

Address ————————————————————————————

————————————————————————————

————————————————————————————

————————————————————————————